McGoorty

•

A
POOL
ROOM
HUSTLER

•

Robert Byrne

LIBRARY OF LARCENY

BROADWAY BOOKS

NEW YORK

First published in 1972 by Lyle Stuart, Inc.

PRINTED IN THE UNITED STATES OF AMERICA

BROADWAY BOOKS and B colophon and Library of Larceny and colophon are trademarks of Random House, Inc.

Visit our website at www.broadwaybooks.com

First Broadway Books trade paperback edition published 2004

The Library of Congress has cataloged the hardcover edition as follows:

McGoorty, Danny, 1901–1970.
McGoorty : a pool room hustler / [as told to] Robert Byrne.
    p.   cm.
Originally published: Secaucus, N.J. : Lyle Stuart, c1972.
Includes index.
1. McGoorty, Danny, 1901–1970.   2. Billiard players—United States—
Biography.   I. Byrne, Robert, 1930–   II. Title.
GV892.2.M38 M36 2000
794.7'2'092—dc21
00-010599

ISBN 0-7679-1631-X

1   3   5   7   9   10   8   6   4   2

To Lillian McGoorty
who suffered most

Contents

Preface to the First Edition

For a student of three-cushion billiards there was no better place to be in 1954 than San Francisco, headquarters of half a dozen world-class players. Most of the action was at The 924 Club, an old-fashioned, faintly seedy billiard parlor that was open to the public but closed to the sun. Thirty years before, when it was known as Graney's Billiard Academy, it was one of the best-equipped and most famous rooms in the country—"the finest," according to Willie Hoppe.

The talent on display was awesome. Welker Cochran and Ray Kilgore played almost every day. Cochran, many times world champion, was past his prime but still impressive; Kilgore had replaced Hoppe as title-holder the year before in Chicago. I sat spellbound for hours watching Masako Katsura, precise and petite, show her mastery of both balk-line and three-cushion.* When she was at the table practicing there was always at least one newcomer among the spectators with an amazed look on his face, dumfounded at the sight of a woman so accomplished in a game thought to be reserved for men.

And there was Danny McGoorty. Deadpan Dan. A pool hustler turned billiard player, he had great natural ability, and despite a history of alcoholism he had many impressive match and tournament victories to his credit. He had won the Pacific Coast Championship in 1947, ahead of Kilgore, and in 1949 surprised the oddsmakers by finishing second to Joe Chamaco of Mexico

---

* See Appendix for a description of three-cushion billiards.

in the United States national tournament, an achievement that gave him a shot at Hoppe's world title.

He had a deep knowledge of the game and approached each shot as an intellectual problem to be solved. In a game he was deliberate and relentless, totally committed to the goal of winning. He executed his shots with a beautiful economy of force, never playing to the audience by hitting the cueball harder than he had to. If he had a technical weakness it was perhaps a tendency to overemphasize defense. At times he seemed unwilling to take offensive risks even when the balls were rolling in his favor.

It wasn't his skill as a player that made him stand out from his competition; it was his personality. He was sarcastic, profane, negative, irritable . . . and uniquely humorous. In the so-called pool-hall subculture, a world well populated with vivid characters, he was the most vivid of all. In every major city today you can find old-timers who knew him and who enjoy trading stories about him. He had little reason to imagine as he did that his enemies were legion and that they were joined in a conspiracy he called The Hate McGoorty Club.

Danny McGoorty was of medium height and build, with brown hair, square shoulders, a square face, and a voice so strong it suggested a carnival barker. Very concerned about his appearance, he was given to wearing conservative suits and glossy shoes, and could have been taken for a bank president or a corporation lawyer. When he spoke, however, he was revealed at once as a man who had spent a lifetime looking at the world from underneath. Around women he respected he changed his image somewhat, cleaned up his language, and became almost courtly, in a rough-around-the-edges way. Many men found him insulting and abrasive, but women, even sophisticated women, saw something undeniably attractive about him. No one who knew him will doubt the tales of amour in this book.

When I first saw McGoorty in 1954 he was 51 years old and for the first time in his life free of the effects of alcohol. He had not touched a drop in two years, and was seriously applying himself to three-cushion billiards in an effort to go as far as he could in the one field he knew before it was too late. Unfortunately, it was already too late; pool and billiards in the United States were entering an almost total eclipse. Within a few years Hoppe, Matsuyama, Cochran and Kilgore were dead, Schaefer, Bozeman, and Katsura were retired, and the great old billiard rooms were closing one after the other for lack of business. The new generation was more interested in television, bowling, and golf. The 1953 tournament in Chicago proved to be the last professional world championship for over thirty years. Danny McGoorty had waited about 10 years too long before pulling himself together; now it was to be his fate to see the game he loved shrink steadily until it almost disappeared.

Because I was anxious to learn whatever I could from players of McGoorty's caliber, I played five or six times a week at The 924 Club and its successor, Palace Billiards, and eventually I got to know him well. Over a period of fifteen years I heard most of his favorite stories and expressions more than once and filled a notebook with them. He had an endless store of anecdotes about his adventures as a pool hustler, hobo, and tournament billiard player, and he was a mine of colorful information about hustlers and champions both famous and obscure.

In 1969 I told him that I would like to interview him some day and write a book about his life. "Why do a thing like that?" he said, looking at me with a characteristic expression of mock amazement. "If what I told you got published they'd lock us both up for life. I tell the truth, you know. I don't pour piss in people's ears." He was interested in the idea, but because there seemed no reason to hurry we didn't pursue it beyond having a talk now and then about what such a book might contain. In 1970 something happened that showed there was a reason to hurry after all.

I met him at the Palace after not seeing him for a month or

two and saw a shocking change in his appearance. He was haggard, underweight, beaten down. For the first time in his life Danny McGoorty looked his age and more, with the posture and movements of a very old man. When he saw me he came right to the point: "If you still want to do that book, we better get started awful sudden, because I've got cancer. Big Casino. One croaker gives me only six months."

I was in his hotel room the next night, and we met there almost daily for the next six weeks. He spoke without the slightest inhibition, ignoring the microphone of my tape recorder, and despite his rapidly failing health he spoke at length. Because he didn't know how much time he had left he went into greatest detail on those parts of his life he knew I wasn't already familiar with. I decided almost from the beginning of our interviews that the best way to capture him in a book was to let him tell his own story in his own words. The way he expressed himself was one of the most important things about him.

At one point he broke off his reminiscences and said, "I know a lot of people who would get their guns off if they saw me in Macy's autographing books. I hope I can stay alive long enough to see this stuff in print."

To my great sorrow, he was never to know that pleasure.

Danny McGoorty was the last active professional billiard player whose career spanned the Golden Age of the game, when Ralph Greenleaf, Willie Hoppe, Jake Schaefer, and Welker Cochran were among the best-known names in American sports. In his last years his sense of humor was edged with bitterness and despair and he became a tragic figure, a man who had spent a lifetime mastering an art that died. Near the end I sometimes found him sitting alone along the wall of a billiard room, without a game to play, without even a game to watch, without a single old-timer to talk to about the great champions and tournaments that once seemed so important.

Ironically, three-cushion billiards in the United States is now showing some signs of life. A modest revival is under way, but it is impossible to imagine the game recovering the popularity it once enjoyed. Even if it did, it wouldn't be the same without Danny McGoorty and the characters who made up his world.

—Robert Byrne
November, 1971
Mill Valley, California

Preface to the 2004 Edition

As I write these lines in the fall of 2003, Danny McGoorty has been gone thirty-three years. I still miss him. He was a genuine character without intending to be. There was nothing more enjoyable than sitting in the bleachers next to him during a pool or billiard tournament, listening to his comments about the players we were watching or the players he had known over the course of his fifty years in and around the game. And there was nothing more depressing than serving as his pallbearer on a cold, rainy day in Seattle.

When I was interviewing McGoorty in his last days, trying to get as much information as I could before he was finished forever, Waterfront Fred—I never knew his last name—called me aside in the old Palace Billiards on Market Street in San Francisco and wondered why I was writing a book about McGoorty. "Bozeman was a much better player," he said. True, and Bozeman was an amusing storyteller, too, but Bozeman hadn't spent years as a road hustler and freight hopper and had never been a reckless boozer and skirt chaser. McGoorty's language, unlike Bozeman's, was rooted in the Roaring Twenties, the hobo jungles of the Great Depression, and the Chicago of the Capone mob years. Listen to McGoorty tell his tales and you'll taste flavors of American social history that you'll never find in a textbook. He had a self-deprecating wit, a brutal honesty, a colorful way of expressing himself, and a willingness to talk about his private life and his failings in terms harsher than his worst critics. There could hardly be a better subject for a biography.

After he told me he had a terminal case of what he called the Big Casino, I began tape-recording his recollections and observations partly because I thought the attention would cheer him up and partly because I thought I might be able to get an article out of it for *Esquire* or *Playboy*. The more he talked, the more I realized that he was giving me the raw material for an unusual book. I'll always be grateful to publisher Lyle Stuart for taking a chance on an unknown writer's tale of travels through a seldom-seen subculture, to the reviewers and readers who viewed it as more than just a book about a game, and now to Broadway Books for bringing McGoorty back for an encore.

Before he died, McGoorty gave me a few items from his small stock of memorabilia. There were a couple of billiards books and pamphlets from the 1920s, a few photographs, a set of ivory billiard balls he kept inside one of his woolen socks. Best of all was a handwritten letter to him from one of the most famous sportsmen in the world, a man whose career as a billiards champion stretched from 1906 to 1952.

Miami Beach, October 11, 1957
Dear Danny:
Your card came this morning. Thanks so much for remembering my birthday. Have been living here for over a year and really like it. Of course, I go north about twice a year to break this hot weather.

Play once in a while and do a little teaching, as I do miss the game of billiards as it's been the greater part of my life. I want to wish you lots of success . . . If I get out there next Spring will drop in to see you . . . I plan to go out and see the children.

Again I thank you for your kindness. Regards to all and yourself.

Willie Hoppe

There's another handwritten letter I treasure. It's from Willie Mosconi, who wrote me after reading the book.

Haddon Heights, New Jersey, July 19, 1972
Dear Bob:
Please accept my sincerest apologies for not replying to your very kind letter of a few weeks ago. The Mrs. and I had to make a visit to Italy to settle her father's estate and we just got back over the weekend. I am glad we agree on one thing, that Fats is a phony. I cannot understand why the magazine writers insist on billing this fraud as a great player. Some of the players of the past should speak out, but unfortunately none of them have so far.

In regards to your book *McGoorty*. My opinion is that it's at times funny, often obscene, occasionally filthy, here and there exaggerated, but it's an entertaining story of a guy who doesn't try to pass himself off as any sort of giant at the table; just a fellow who loved the game. In general, a great book. I wish you the best of luck with it. I will certainly push and recommend it wherever I go.

Sincerely yours,
Willie Mosconi

P.S. I am also penning a book at the present telling of my experiences with the players of my era and also of the phonies, including Fats, of that time. In general, an expose of the creeps that I have known over the years. Best of luck once again.

More than one poolhall denizen told me that not only was *McGoorty* the best book they had ever read, it was the only book they had ever read. Some chipped in with anecdotes, like the old-timer who told me he once handed an expensive cue he had just bought to Danny, whom he barely knew, and asked for his opinion. He looked it over carefully, checked the straightness and stiffness, examined the tip, the joint, and the wrap. He handed it back to the owner and asked in his deadpan way, "Does the Better Business Bureau know about this?"

There were other letters. Two were written by McGoorty in 1969 to an old friend in Chicago, Bandylegs Goodman, who sent them to me. One begins:

Dear Marvin:
My home address now is 835 Turk Street, San Francisco. It's a residential hotel, now known as a key joint since they discarded the telephone switchboard, the clerks, the bellboys, and the whores.

The other begins:

Dear Marvin:
What's happening besides the rent? I didn't answer your letter sooner because, as you put it, we aren't going steady. Well, enough of that bullshit.

I'll take the last sentiment as my cue to step off stage and let the show begin.

Robert Byrne
November 2003
Dubuque, Iowa

"I remember McGoorty in Chicago in the 1920s. Drunk all the time."

—Chinatown Jimmy

"McGoorty was championship timber, but he gave the dolls and refreshments first call."

—Bob McCarty,
in the *Sacramento Union*

"He came into my billiard room and asked for a job. I said, 'McGoorty, I'll give you fifty bucks a month if you just stay out of the joint.'"

—Big Red Powers

"His control of cueball speed was so beautiful I drool when I think of it."

—Short Gordon

"He was a handsome dude, and quite a fashion plate."

—Bandylegs Goodman

"His eyes light up and his voice grows louder when he recalls his happier experiences."

—Jack Olsen,
in *Sports Illustrated*

"He should have been a nightclub comedian."

—Ratface

"I never cared much for the guy. But I miss him."

—Waterfront Fred

McGoorty

Part One

•

GROWING UP DRUNK

1901–1929

i
Choosing a Career

If you think the Chicago cops are bad now, you should have seen them in the 1920's . . . my God, nobody was safe! They used to follow me all around the Loop, back and forth across the streets, in and out of restaurants. Into pool halls they followed me, right into the toilets. "Let's see your identification. Where do you work? Why not? Where do you live? How much money you got on you?" If I had a five-dollar bill I would have to fork it over to keep from getting thrown in the bucket for vagrancy. Then the next day those red-faced pricks would nail me again.

What bothered them about me was that I had no job and showed no signs of wanting to get one. They just could not stand the idea of a young man like me not having a job, and they weren't the only ones—my aunts were riding me about it, too. I was living with my aunts Margaret and Kate because they didn't charge me any rent and because they were good cover. When I told the cops I lived with two square apples in a nice residential neighborhood they figured I must be at least some kind of half-ass family man.

For a couple of years I had my aunts believing that I was spending all my time looking for work. They even gave me carfare and lunch money to make it easier. But they smartened up finally and told me I had to get a job and quit making excuses. They were not going to keep on supporting me, they said, if I was idling instead of choosing a career.

Pool hustler, that's the career I was choosing, although I didn't think of it that way at the time. All I knew was that playing pool was the only thing I liked to do. Day and night I studied the top Chicago players, watched how they controlled the cueball, how they played defense, how they hustled babies like me. There was money being made, a lot of money, and I was sure I could get good enough to get my share if I worked at it. I kept my eyes and ears wide open and I practiced every day until my arm was like lead. I don't call that idling.

As far back as I can remember I have been fascinated by pool and billiards. As a kid in San Francisco I used to skip school a week at a time and do nothing but stare through the windows of pool halls. What I saw was paradise: guys who didn't have to wear knickers, who played pool all the time, laughing and gambling and bullshitting. There was a Greek joint on Kearny Street that I liked because I could sometimes sneak in and take a few shots— this was in about 1916, when I was only fifteen years old. Usually before I had time to chalk my cue the chief Greek had me by the ass of the pants and was slinging me through the door. I can still feel myself getting hoisted by the crotch and run across the floor on my tiptoes. In a year's time I gave that Greek a hell of a workout. He finally said I could stay, but only if I was with my father. My father had left the picture years before—he just walked out, my mother said—so I had to spend my school lunch money to hire one, which was no problem. Every pool hall had practically a regular staff of old geezers sitting around soaking up the heat, and whenever I showed up with change jingling in my pocket a dozen of them got to their feet and volunteered to be dad.

I lived with my mother in those days, a fine-looking woman with brown hair that hung clear down past her keester. She was on the road a lot, peddling a line of foot powder and stockings, but when she was in town she did her best to raise me right. She took me to the opera about nineteen thousand times on the theory that it would make me more refined. Even when I was real little she dragged me down the aisle of that fucking opera house to hear a bunch of Italians holler stuff neither of us could understand. Afterwards she always took me to a beer garden on Powell Street and made me dance with her. I squawked like hell about learning how to dance. I didn't realize how much help it would be to me later with the broads.

As far as broads were concerned, I was seventeen years old before I was able to get my finger damp enough to turn a page. Once I got started, though, I became quite the little cocksman. It was the pelvis bumping, in fact, and not the pool playing that finished me with my mother. She found a rubber in my pocket one day and that was the end of it. She said she was on the road too much to keep an eye on me and that she was going to have to send me to Chicago to live with my aunts, who could give me a proper home life. Jesus Christ, that was a terrible mistake from her point of view. San Francisco was like kindergarten compared to Chicago. I don't know what my mother should have done, but sending me to Chicago was not it.

When my aunts told me I had to get a job I surprised them by getting a dozen right off the bat, but I didn't last long on any of them because the pay was so lousy. I usually did all right until I saw the first paycheck, then I would tell everybody off. "You mean this is all I get for hanging around here since Tuesday?

Why, I can make more than this out picking shit with the chickens." If I didn't get canned then, I would after calling in sick a few times from pool halls.

I have always hated working. A job to me is . . . well, it's an invasion of privacy. Getting blasted out of bed by an alarm clock so you can go somewhere and do things you don't want to do, that's not my idea of living. Assembling parts and selling soda pop and delivering packages made me feel like a goddam dummy.

My aunts got so fed up they called in an expert, a cousin of mine who was a police captain. He considered himself a champion at choosing careers for people, and I have to admit that with him on the scene I got a better class of job. He knew how to pull strings. It was his idea that I would be much steadier if I worked for the city. All he had to do was make one phone call and I was on the payroll. He called somebody in the Traffic Bureau, which ran the streetcars, buses, and elevated trains.

"I'm sending a relative of mine over," he said. "He starts tomorrow."

Before I was through I worked in every department the Traffic Bureau had. I collected nickels on the ass-end of streetcars, I closed air-powered doors on people in train stations, and I drove a bus through every red light between Jackson and State in the Loop and Devon Avenue, which is 6500 north. I needed a chauffeur's license to be a bus driver, but I didn't have to take a test or anything—my cousin just wrote one out for me. I drove that bus for fourteen months, which is the longest I have ever stayed on one job in my entire life. The reason I was such a faithful employee was that I wore a uniform and some broad told me I looked cute in it.

But all those city jobs interfered too much with my billiard playing, so I moved into another area of transportation: cab driving. Whenever I got hard up for money I went to work for one of the cab companies, starting with Red Top and going through Premier, Yellow, and Checker. Shamrock Eakin, one of my pals from those years, got to calling me Transportation Dan, a name that stuck with me for a long time because it took me quite a while to go through all the cab companies in town.

As a cab driver I was a good competitor. I fought hard, crashed fenders to get to the hotel doorman first, and got my nose busted by other cabbies more than once. The main thing I didn't like about it was the worry about getting robbed or mugged. One night at 43rd and Cottage Grove I picked up a guy who gave me an address that as near as I could figure was an empty lot next to a railroad bridge. Well, I thought to myself, it is going to be a heist. I am going to be heisted at last. As we went along I slipped my big bills real slow into my shoes and under the seat, trying not to move my shoulders or my head. With my foot I slid the jack handle across the floor to where I could grab it fast if I had to. For all I knew he had a gun on me all the time. When we got to the address I pulled over to the curb and said, "Will this be good enough, sir?" It was pitch black, but there were some lights about half a block away.

"Yeah," he said, "this is perfect."

I rang the meter and tore off the ticket that showed the fare—eighty-five cents—and handed it back to him. Instead of slipping me some cold steel he gave me a bill and got out of the cab. As he walked away I turned on my spotlight to see what I had in my hand. It was a sawbuck—a ten. How do you like that? I thought it was a heist and I wound up making $9.15 on the deal.

A lot of my customers asked me to find them a girl. When I heard that, I drove out to the Rex, or Capone's joint, the Four Deuces. The cabbie always got forty percent of whatever the guy spent. You took the guy up to the front door as if you had to introduce him to the bouncer. "This is my cousin Joe from Kokomo. Fix him up." The reason you walked to the door was so the bouncer could get the number off your cap. Next time you showed up he paid you off. They were very fair about paying off because they wanted the cabbies bird dogging for them.

The most fantastic thing in the world happened to me one night when I was driving a cab. A very sharp-looking uppercrust broad hailed me on 47th Street. She was wearing a squirrel-skin coat with tassels on the bottom that touched the ground, and under that she had on a shiny evening gown. Strictly class.

"Go over 47th," she said, so I did. At about Wentworth she said, "Turn left here." It was a dark street and I had to cut the speed way down. In the middle of the block, where there was no streetlight, she told me to stop. I was getting a little worried, because some of the broads were heisters, too. Soon as I pulled over she put her hand on my shoulder. "Why don't you come back here and have a smoke with me?" she said.

I left the meter running and got in the back seat. I sat next to her and nobody said a word. Then all of a sudden I'll be a sonofabitch if she didn't go down on me and start blowing my wazzle. She didn't do it to beat the fare, either, because when I let her out on Halsted later she paid me in full. It was just one of those once-in-a-lifetime things. I climbed into the back seat and sat next to her without making any kind of a move. She puffed away on a cigarette for about a minute, then she said, "Well, I might as well try it," and started unbuttoning me. I didn't give her any help at all and she had quite a bit of trouble. There were no zippers in those days. Zippers came in a lot later. People don't realize that. An odd thing about this dame was that she really didn't know how to blow a wazzle. She was no professional at it, that's for sure. She was just getting even with some guy or getting ready for him.

The minute I was free I made a beeline for the nearest cab station. There used to be at least two hundred cab stations in Chicago, little offices with a call box where you could go in and get warm and spit on the stove. When I got there I counted eleven cabs ahead of me, but after the boys heard what had happened to me they moved me to the head of the line. They enjoyed the story so much they made me first out.

If things like that happened every night I would probably still be a cab driver today, but usually the job was pretty boring. You could make good money if you put in the hours, but I took too much time off. The green felt. I would practically double-park my cab on Randolph Street to play billiards. The green felt cost me every job I ever had.

One thing has always puzzled me. Why do people feel so bad when they lose a job? It made me feel happy as hell, and I always celebrated with a few drinks. When you get a job, that's when you should have the long face. You need a few drinks then, too.

My aunts gave up on me finally and kicked me out, just as my mother had before them. I didn't care. I couldn't stay sober and I couldn't keep a job, but I had improved so much as a pool player that I could make almost as much hustling as I could working. I moved into a cheap hotel. I can remember waking up there one afternoon with a terrific hangover. I stared at the ceiling for a long time, and then I said to myself, "McGoorty, what you have turned out to be is a two-bit, drunken pool hustler." That didn't depress me at all. Listen, I was glad to have a profession.

2

Handbook
for
Hustlers

By 1923 the Chicago hustlers were leaving me alone. I was one of them. It was in 1923 that I got a run of seventy-four balls in rack pool. That may not sound like much today, but it was on a five-by-ten-foot table with four-inch corner pockets and two-and-a-quarter-inch balls. The world tournament record on that kind of equipment was only eighty-five. The tables they use today are smaller and have bigger pockets, which changes the game entirely. Now it's all offense. The promoters did that. They wanted more scoring and longer runs for the spectators.

When you are hustling, naturally, you never make a long run. You never show what you can really do. I got to be a good hustler, and if I had been a little smarter about broads and booze I could have made a decent living at it. As it was I was usually broke and was always having to take some goddam job for a few weeks to bail myself out. Pool hustling is a very tough line of work. If you expect to make anything you not only have to be a good player, you have to be a psychologist, an actor, and a thief as well.

There was a fantastic number of places to hustle pool in. Believe it or not, in the early 1920's in Cook County, Illinois, there were 5,200 licensed pool halls. A lot of them were one- and two-table joints in barber shops and cigar stores and so on, but that is the number of licenses there were, and shows how popular the game used to be. In the Chicago Loop alone—where there is not a single poolroom today—there were twelve big layouts, each one with no less than forty tables. Augie Kieckhefer's place at 18 East Randolph Street, which was pretty much my headquarters, had fifty-five tables on one floor—forty were billiards, the rest pool and snooker.

I had a regular route I used to take looking for suckers to rob. The twelve rooms in the Loop were within walking distance of each other. There was the room at 131 South Wabash, there was the Blackhawk at Randolph and Wabash, around the corner was 18 East Randolph, down the line was 53 Randolph. Underneath the Woods Theatre was a very nice room. Down around South State Street—Van Buren, Jackson, in through there—were quite a few rooms, but a little on the rough side, with fights and what have you. Most of the Loop rooms were run with an iron hand; no vulgarity or rowdyism or hollering allowed. They did a terrific business in the afternoons, when they were crowded with businessmen, salesmen, people who could take long lunch hours, goldbrickers of various sorts. If you walked in at three in the afternoon you almost always had to get on a waiting list for a table. In the evenings, though, business dropped way off, so us hustlers had to get out of the downtown area and scout the suburbs.

There were quite a few of us hustling at the same time, so we had to split up, spread out, make different moves. One would go southeast, another south, another north, even though north meant going all the way to Wilson and Sheridan. You couldn't just hang around on street corners or the cops would vag you. You had to keep on the go, carrying a newspaper with a few classified ads circled so you could say you were looking for a job. Standing on a street corner you better have a bus transfer in your hand.

So we kept moving on our routes, going from room to room. In case a mark wandered into a place when we weren't there, one of our bird dogs would phone us. I had a bird dog in almost every "action" room who would tip me off for small change. If a couple of us were sitting in a room when a mark walked in we would sometimes draw straws to see who got first crack at him.

There is one thing I want to throw in here. In all the hustling I've done I've never seen what you would call a code of ethics. Unless they are teamed up in some kind of swindle, hustlers are usually strictly out for themselves. I've had them come right up to my table when I am playing and say to my mark, "You gonna keep playing him? You got no chance in the world." Trying to spoil my action, trying to get the guy for themselves.

Marks aren't easy to find, and once you get hold of one it's quite an art to make the biggest possible score. There are a million tricks. You never make a tough shot, unless you can make it look lucky. Miscuing five times in a game of rotation is par . . . not just any miscue, but a miscue that leaves no shot. Miscuing properly, so that it looks accidental and so that the cueball goes where you want it to, is a tough thing to learn. But it is a good weapon, even in billiards, where you can get a good leave without being charged with an intentional safety.

If the guy looks like a real dummy, I might play left-handed, or use a crooked stroke, or stand with the wrong foot forward. Instead of making a solid, professional-looking bridge for the cue with my left hand, I might just lay it over the back of my hand—the "fuck-knuckle grip," we used to call it.

Unless you are fishing for big game it is no good to carry your own cue into a room. The small fry button their pockets when they see a guy screwing a fancy cue together. In the big Loop rooms there was no need for a private cue . . . the house cues were beautiful and kept in perfect condition. If you are in some jerkwater town, where the house cues are mop handles and broomsticks, then it is nice to have your own cue, but you don't carry it in—you send somebody else in with it first, who then "loans" it to you later. Or you can do like Johnny Irish, or The Eufala Kid, or Washington Rags: stick the cue into the shithouse through the window, then come around and walk in the front door without it. Anything but walk in with it.

Sometimes it is a tricky proposition to get a mark to play for money at all. A way that worked many times for me was to offer to play a game of rotation "for fun." I would set him up for the one-ball, and when he made it I would hand him a dime, saying that by "for fun" I meant a dime on every odd ball. Not many guys could turn down that dime. Once they took it, naturally, I could go ahead and make the rest of the odd balls.

If you have time and can afford it, it pays to lose a dollar or two before starting to win. There is a risk connected with that, though. I walked into Kieckhefer's one day and Sam, a junky that hung around there, rushed up to me all excited.

"He's in the can, he's in the can . . ." he said.

"Sam," I said, "calm down. Who is in the can?"

"A mark . . . a mark is in the can. Let him win the first game and he is good for a hundred."

I had only four dollars to my name at the time, but I took his advice and dropped the first game for a deuce, which wasn't easy, because the guy could hardly play at all. I had to jump the cue-ball off the table, miscue, hit the wrong ball, every fucking thing to lose. When he finally slopped in the game ball, he picked up my money and walked out of the joint! That finished me with Sam. After that I never gave him change for a wet match. I learned a lesson, though, and that was to win the first game, making it look lucky. Then I could throw a game on the other guy's money.

Losing games and missing shots on purpose . . . you have to have acting ability to make it look convincing. The main trick to hustling is to never make a hard shot or a high run. Make two or three, then miss as if by accident, leaving the guy a tough shot. Stall until he leaves a shot you can make without showing anything.

You can work a room for two or three days if you aren't known, or even longer, climbing up to the better players as the bums drop off. But when you finally get to the local shark you still have to hide your stuff, because the guys you beat the day before might wise up and get a little unhappy if they see your true speed.

In three-cushion billiards a good way to hide part of your ability is to shoot into kisses. Try your best to get a kiss off the second or third rail. Even top players usually won't suspect you are doing it on purpose. I learned that a long time ago from a man by the name of Bruce Pierce.

In a strange room, by far the best way to stir up some action is to spend a day losing money while the local boys are watching. When you come in the next day they'll jump on you like a bunch of horny monkeys.

Myself, I never seemed to have the money to invest in a losing day. Often as not I would have a snootful of booze and challenge the best player in the joint right off the bat. Now that is not as stupid as it sounds, because the town champ almost has to call your bluff if he wants to hold his head up with his cronies, and you can play for good stakes right away instead of fooling around with nickels and dimes.

Some hustlers I knew were terrific actors. You would swear they were drunk, or sick, or just learning to play. Tugboat Whaley used to put on rain gear, rubber hat and all, and say he was a tugboat captain who had just retired on a nice pension that he didn't know how to spend. Wimpy Lassiter, before the tournament prizes got big enough to draw him into the limelight, dressed up like a hillbilly, with bib overalls and a piece of straw a foot long hanging off his lip. That was his hustle, pretending he just fell off a hay wagon. The hillbilly lingo he talked, though, was no con . . . that was the way he really did talk. He would wander in a room and try to get a game of "bounce pool, like we play in South Carolina." By that he meant bank pool, where you have to bank every ball. He was a master at it. When I first saw Wimpy in his uniform I like to shit . . . the straw hat he had on! It was a work of art the way it had been chewed on . . . just enough to fringe it. He drank quite a bit, but never enough to lose his taw, his entry fee into the action.

There usually are two or three guys going around the country pretending to be rich Texas cattle ranchers ready to lose a bundle. Here's how that act goes. The hustler walks into a room and stops just inside the door. He is wearing a two-hundred-dollar buckskin coat, a ten-gallon Stetson, and fancy hundred-dollar boots. He makes a big show of lighting a cigar as he looks around, maybe using two or three big kitchen matches. When he is sure everybody in the joint is looking at him, he shakes out the match, blows a long funnel of smoke, and says: "Well, boys, I came to play."

If that doesn't generate some business he can try counting his money, which always seems to work like magic. He goes over to a table that all the customers can see and lays out his cash, making piles, starting with the fifties and hundreds, working down to the fives and tens, until there is beautiful money all over. If there is anybody in the room who can hold a cue, he will want to take a crack at some of that loot, and if he is chicken he will want to see somebody else do it. There will be guys grabbing phones and flying out the doors and windows, trying to get hold of Toledo Slim or Marvin the Mailman, anybody who can play a lick. It's the sight of the money. It does something to people. They do things they shouldn't.

Winning is never a sure thing, no matter how good you get. I was playing awful good pool in 1923 and 1924. On a four-and-a-half-by-nine table I sometimes played rack pool fifty or no count, meaning that I had to run fifty balls in a row before I could put anything on the wire. Even so, there was a guy that showed up in Kieckhefer's who gave me fits. I played him six games a day for a week. I would win the first three, he would win the second three. We were getting nowhere, just handing money over to the house for table time. Then I noticed that he always went into the can after the third game. And I noticed that the toilet didn't flush. He was going in there to pop pills or smoke weed or some damned thing! When he came out he shot the shit out of the balls. To beat him, I decided, I would have to bar him from the can.

"Listen," I said, "no more going to the can. It breaks my stroke and throws me off my game. Sitting around waiting for you I get cold. You don't see me going to the can in the middle of the session. Take a piss like I do, before we start." Oh, I gave him quite a bit of shit.

"Fuck you, you asshole," he said. "I'll go to the can whenever the hell I want to. If you want to play, okay; if you don't, that's okay, too."

So we didn't play. There was no percentage in playing the guy if he could go to the can. And I wasn't interested in playing hee-haw . . . for the fun of it.

That guy was one of the few I ever met who could play better when he was juiced, or doped. Another was Clarence Gifford. With a shot in the arm he was liable to run two hundred balls. But most guys who try it only think they are playing better. They don't have near the sharpness and touch they had before.

Early in my career I had the misfortune of taking a few drinks in the middle of a tough game and then coming from behind to win. I thought I had stumbled onto a secret: I could settle my nerves by swilling a little giggle-soup. I started going to the can in the middle of every game to suck on a bottle. Before long I was overdoing it, and when I came out of the can I could hardly remember what table I was playing on. When I found it I had to hang onto the rails to stand up. My nerves were settled, yeah, but I didn't know what the fuck I was doing.

Thank God I never got into the dope thing. I tried smoking marijuana once but nothing happened.

"How do you feel?" the guy asked who gave it to me.

"I don't feel nothing."

"You don't feel nothing?"

"No."

"Take another drag. Deep, and hold it."

I did. Nothing.

"You aren't getting high? You aren't feeling a little something?"

"No."

"Then don't waste it," he said, and he grabbed it away from me.

Plenty of times I played for money when I didn't have any, which is called playing on your nerve. When you do that you absolutely have to win. You can't show any mercy, or give the other guy any chance at all. All good hustlers and tournament players have the killer instinct, and the way they get it is by playing on their nerve a few times. A lot of good players never get to the top because when they get ahead in a game they start feeling sorry for their opponent. They ease up on him instead of kicking him when he is down. Players who do that have never had to play for their breakfast. You've got to look at it this way: If you are playing your grandmother a fifty-point game, try to beat her fifty to nothing. Or if you have her forty-nine to three, try to keep her from getting to four. Try to hate her. It helps to hate whoever you are playing, which has never been any problem for me. I don't know how much talent I have, but I have a lot of natural hate. A guy by the name of Rusty Jones told me that a great many players are killers and haters, but with me the hate shows through.

"When you bend over that table, McGoorty," he said, "you look like a killer."

A few more things about hustling. Just as much money changes hands between the "sweaters"—the spectators—as between the players, and that is where the real treachery comes in, because the players might be in cahoots. Now when the best player throws the game it is called a dump. The next level is the double dump, where the mark thinks he is in on a fix and then is double-crossed. There is even the double double dump, where a guy thinks he has been let in on a plan to double-cross a mark who thinks he knows a fix is on, only to be double-crossed himself. All the players do is make the game come out so that their secret partner on the sidelines wins his bet. I've seen guys go to a lot of trouble to arrange a fix only to find out that they were the marks all along.

Some hustlers work alone, others use a partner. I did it both ways. A partner is a good way to wake up a dead room. He goes in first, plays a game or two, or just sits around. When you come in an hour later he hits you up for a game, then quits after losing a few bucks. You both play terrible. On the sidelines he whispers to some asshole, "You can beat that prick, he can't play at all. Go ahead, play him for ten a game . . . I'll take half your action. You can work him for plenty."

Another way to use a partner is to win or lose small bets at the table while he is winning big bets on the sidelines. If he bets against you, you lose. If he bets for you, you win. But not every time, naturally.

But using partners and pulling dumps and double dumps and all that stuff—the lemonade, it is called—is bunco, real con. In fact, all hustling, where you hide your speed, is stealing. You might just as well pick the guy's pocket or bust into his home. I quit doing it as soon as I could afford to, which was about thirty years later.

I was on the receiving end one time when somebody else was

lemonading. A guy came into the Woodlawn Recreation in Chicago, where I was sitting on my rosette doing nothing, and said to me, "Come on, let's play some snooker."

"I don't play snooker," I said.

Then he whispered, "Play me a couple of games. I'll fatten you up."

We played and he lost twenty-eight bucks to me. What I didn't know was that there was a Mark Anthony—that's a super-sucker—on the sidelines. The game was being staged for his benefit. At closing time my opponent said in a loud voice, "I'll be back tomorrow night with more money." He was, too, but not to play me. He played Mark Anthony and took him for eight hundred dollars. He was just using me the day before to make himself look like a loser.

Even in the twenties, when times were good and pool was a major sport, it was just about impossible to make a living by hustling alone. Most of the hustlers I knew had something else going for them. Maybe their old ladies slung hash or peddled their boxes, or they themselves were some kind of thieves. Like Bert Parno. He got a call from a bird dog one day about some one-pocket action on the north side. I didn't play one-pocket myself, but I decided to go along for the entertainment. We didn't have a car, so we got on a rattler, which was jammed. After I paid my fare I looked around and saw Bert standing real close to some poor bastard and practically sticking a newspaper in his nose. "Oh, no," I thought to myself, "not *that* . . . he's not going to do *that* . . ." But he did do it. He lifted the guy's wallet. I fought my way through the people to the other end of the car . . . I wanted no part of what was going on.

When we got to the other room and stepped off the elevator, Bert waved me into the can, where he took a look at what he got. "Why that cheap sonofabitch," he said, taking the money out, "seven lousy bucks." He snapped the billfold shut, and with all the personal stuff and identification still in it he sailed it out the window, clear over on top of some other fucking building. After that I never even walked down the street with Bert Parno.

Another case was "Fat Willie" Kiefer, a great big guy whose nose was always running. A slob. He was a deputy sheriff for Cook County and one of the worst crooks in town. Steal money right out of your pocket, if he could. Pull his star on you if he thought it would throw you off your game. He was so cheap he would do anything to get out of paying for rides on buses or subways. I was with him once when he climbed over an electric fence to get on the Jackson Park El. All that trouble to beat the city of Chicago out of a lousy dime. The thing about it was that at all times he had six thousand-dollar bills pinned to his shorts. I know, because he showed them to me once in a shithouse, which was kind of an honor because when he put his money away it almost never saw daylight again. He was a good player . . . in rack pool Fat Willie could shoot the lights out.

It takes nerve to be a crook, but you have to be half nuts, too. It is suicidal. You can't keep it up. The more you get away with the more you try, and you are going to get caught sooner or later. In the big time, now that is a different story entirely, because other people do the dirty work for you. But the small stuff, the burglaries and holdups and so on, I could never see it. The percentages are just not there.

Maybe it is true what Shamrock Eakin used to say about me. "Look at that goddam McGoorty—too lazy to work and too yellow to steal."

3

Sex—Free
and Paid

The best place to find broads was in the public dance halls. I was a very good dancer, maybe because of the early coaching my mother gave me in San Francisco. I never got into the championship class, but when they had local contests I was usually in the money.

I could have had a different bag every night if I wanted to, and not because I was cute; the reason was that I could dance. Even ugly good dancers made out almost at will. The girls would wave across the floor to you, holding up fingers to show which dances they still had open. You were considered quite a flop if you went into the Trianon or the Midway Gardens and didn't come out with a tomato.

I didn't always feel like scoring. Some of those broads, especially the ones who sweat a lot and started out the evening covered with perfume and powder . . . why, holy Christ, after sixteen dances they had an odor that would knock your hat off.

Of course, I was probably no rose myself, but that's not for me to say. All I know is that I sometimes didn't have a hell of a lot of desire.

Now and then I was what was called a dinner-pail pimp, which means that I tried to live off working girls. A regular pimp has a girl who sells her body and gives him the money. A dinner-pail pimp keeps her body for himself and makes her work for the groceries to boot. At those dances we were usually trying to pick up a girl, yes, but the trick was to pick one up who not only would go with you to a hotel but would pay the bill and buy breakfast, too. That sounds impossible, but I did it many times. Out on the dance floor, bumping pelvis bones, that's when you found out if a girl had any money, if she seemed willing to spend some of it, if she lived alone, and whatnot.

I broke a good many virgins. The boys considered that a very smart thing to do, but I am ashamed of it now. The only time you can be proud of busting a virgin is if she asks you to, or if she is a prick-teaser. Oh, what some of those broads would do to tease you . . . suck tongues, blow in your ear, rub your organ, then send you home to run a batch off by hand. A guy who busts a broad like that deserves a medal.

You have to admit that a virgin is a challenge. If you can score where twenty other guys have struck out, you've done something. I seemed to have the idea that I *had* to conquer them, prove to them that I was a man and could make them knuckle under. The maidenhead was a barrier that had to be torn down, that *should* be torn down. Somebody was going to do it sooner or later, so it might as well be me and it might as well be now.

But it was so much work! You had to teach them, those virgins, tell them what to do. None of them knew how to keep their asses off the sheets. I want a broad to get her ass up, because I don't have much and I want it to stay there. And you had to keep them from squealing and squawking and worrying about the blood. When it was over they hated you, but that usually didn't last long. I don't know why I went to all the trouble. It was a hell of a lot of grief and it more often than not wasn't much fun. I just had that need to conquer. I must have been ashamed of myself even then, because when I busted a virgin I didn't go around crowing about it like a lot of assholes I knew. I will give myself credit for that.

Some guys are awful big talkers. They claim that they get their gun off six or seven times in one night. When I hear somebody say that he has even been in that many times in one night, I always look him right in the eye and say, "Oh, yeah? How many times with the prick and how many times with the finger?" Because I don't think it is humanly possible. The most I ever came in one night was three, and the third time was about eight hours after the first. Not only that, but after the third time I felt like I'd been scraped out inside by forty WPA workers.

When I was living with my aunts I sometimes tried to sneak girls through the window into my room, but that didn't work out very often—I almost always tripped on the lamp cord or knocked over a chair. "What's going on in there, Dan, my boy?" my aunts would say, which meant that I had to push the girl back out through the window. About twice out of the twenty or so times that I tried to use my room did I actually get the broad on the chopping block—the work bench—and get the job done.

If my aunts had known what I was up to they would have had six kinds of fits. They were very strait-laced and religious. When they had to come out on the sidewalk at three in the morning to pay my cab bill they would ask me when I had been to communion last.

The broads wanted you to wear a rubber, but I hated them. To me, wearing a rubber was like jacking off with boxing gloves. I always made a big show of putting a rubber on, but by hooking a thumb under the rim I could slip it off on the first backstroke. Oh, I was a nice guy in those days. You think I am a turd now!

Rubbers were messy, that was another thing. I ruined a suit once by stuffing one in my pants pocket after a session on the back seat of a car. I don't mean in the back of a car . . . we took the back seat out and put it on the ground in the park so we wouldn't have to lie on the grass.

Mabel, Becky, and Agnes. That was the name of the condoms. That was actually the name. Three for a quarter in a little flat can. You would say to the druggist, "I want Mabel, Becky, and Agnes." The lid had pictures of three girls on it. When fish skins came in they almost put rubbers out of business because they were so much thinner and lighter. They let more feel and warmth through, but I didn't like them much better. It was like screwing a knothole, as far as I was concerned. The broads couldn't tell if you had one on or not, and they were always glancing down to see if you did.

I knocked up a few people. I knocked one broad up five times. Seems like all I had to do was hang my pants on the bedpost and she was pregnant again. I began to wonder if maybe I wasn't the only one getting on base, but she swore and screamed and I believed her. She was a very sincere type of broad. A couple of others claimed I knocked them up, but I figured they were just trying to play position on me.

Five times I took this one broad to an abortionist that was called The Butcher. Fat, red-faced, crude—if he had worn a bloody apron the picture would have been complete. I wish I had a picture of him. Anybody looking at it would say right away, "There is The Butcher."

The Butcher had a very poor bedside manner. I would knock on the door of his house with the broad at my side. He would open the door a crack and say, "Whaddya want?"

"My wife and I, we . . . well . . . she . . ."

"I'm busy. Don't bother me."

So we would wander around on the streets for awhile and try him again later. It was tough to find an abortionist who didn't charge a fortune. There was a war on against abortionists in Chicago at all times. Being a mobster, though, was perfectly all right. The Butcher's rate was fifty dollars. Not forty-nine ninety-five—fifty flat. And in advance. Besides that, you practically had to have a letter of recommendation from Calvin Coolidge.

I eventually quit seeing that girl altogether. We weren't meant for each other. I wouldn't wear a rubber and she was not fond of The Butcher. She got so that when we were screwing she would twist out of the way right at the magic moment, which is absolutely the worst thing that can happen to you. It's enough to drive a man back to his boxing gloves.

When I knocked somebody up my stock sank at the dance halls, but after a few months the broads would take chances on me again, or there would be some new faces. And I must say that it was well known that I stuck by any broad I got in trouble. I didn't run out on them. I gave them a free trip to The Butcher and I was sitting on the curb waiting for them when it was over. I married two of them, for chrissakes.

Even though I got plenty free, I still went to whorehouses now and then. A gang of guys could go to a whorehouse and have a hell of a time. Sometimes at a dance you couldn't find what you wanted or you didn't feel like working for it, so you would go outside to where cabs were waiting to take you to Stickney or Blue Island, where Capone, the Guziks, or Miles O'Donnell had houses. Eight or ten of us might pile into one of those big limousines.

I forget the name of the joint I used to go to most, but I remember the huge main parlor, with chairs against the walls all the way around. There were a hundred girls at least to choose from . . . fat ones, skinny ones, pretty ones, ugly ones, double ugly ones, even. Some guys . . . I don't know, they want all kinds of women. When you picked one out you paid the madam at the bottom of the stairs and she gave you a towel as you went up.

If the guys took too much time looking over the merchandise, the girls would put on a little show. Two would go for each other, one picking an olive out of the other one's pussy. The guys started rushing for the stairs then! Or a girl would pick a guy out of the audience—it was always a pimp, but she would let on that he was just an average tourist—pull his johnny out of his pants and start treating it like a lollipop. That would send a stampede up the stairs, too.

Naturally, the way I carried on, I got a dose of v.d. I woke up one morning with a sticky feeling in my pajamas and I found traces of a discharge. I must have strained myself, I thought, lifting a pool table or some goddam thing. You can get a discharge from straining yourself, you know. Or if a girl gets you all heated up and then leaves you high and dry, something might leak out later. But this particular discharge wouldn't quit. After a few days I got so worried about it that I decided to show it to an old guy in the poolroom who was a sort of connoisseur of venereal diseases. He looked me over in the shithouse. "Probably just a strain, huh?" I said.

"Yeah, it looks like a strain to me. You just strained yourself. Nothing to worry about."

A week later the strain was still with me, so I decided to find out what it was once and for all. I got on an elevated train and went down to the Board of Health on Clark Street. A nurse took me into a big room that had a long row of booths with swinging doors along one wall. She told me to stand in one with my pants at half mast and wait for a doctor, which I did. After a long time of listening to the doctor coming down the line, going from stall to stall, he finally got to me. The doors burst open and there he was.

"All right, all right," he says, "what have we got here? Come on, come on, squeeze it out."

He wants me to milk my cock.

"Well, what are you waiting for?" he says.

I am nervous as hell, but I finally manage to squeeze out a

drop . . . a yellow teardrop. I look up at him and say, "Just a strain, huh, doc?"

"Yeah," he says, "just a strain commonly known as gonorrhea. Got any money?"

I had a little, so he wrote out a prescription for a syringe and some kind of salve, which I had to squirt right into the end of my cock day after day. Oh, man, that was miserable. It took me four months to dry that bug up, and I lived like a monk the whole time. I had many a hard-on, but usually it was because of a stricture. Now a stricture is when some of the discharge clogs up inside and causes a kind of kink in your prick. It is something a doctor has to take care of and sometimes he takes care of it with a rubber mallet. He lays your cock in his hand and says, "Look over there!" And when you look over there he whacks the sonofabitch with the hammer and, my God, pus and blood spurt all over the place. People look at me today when I tell them this and say, "McGoorty, you stupid bastard, no doctor would ever do such a thing." But goddammit, I've had one do it to me. At least, he said he was a doctor. In the old days, before they had such powerful drugs, it was either the rubber mallet or taking a sound, where they run a thing up inside you. I feel awful sorry for any poor guy who has to have a sound taken. It was never done to me, and for that I have always been thankful.

Think how easy it is today. The doctor just gives you a shot of penicillin and you don't have clap or syph any more. Kids today don't know what hell is.

4

Three
Cushions

Bums play pool, gentlemen play billiards. It was as true fifty years ago as it is today. Walk in any room that has both pool and billiard tables and look at the difference between the players. All of the jerks, drifters, bums, hoodlums, loudmouths, and pimps will be playing pool. The guys playing billiards will be a different sort entirely, doctors and dentists, businessmen, professional people, serious-minded types. Sure, you can find college professors playing pool and cornholers playing billiards, but I am talking about the average. Why is this? The way I figure it, billiards is a tougher game . . . you have to be a good pool player to even think about playing billiards, so only those with some staying power get from one game to the other. And there is something about the games themselves that sorts people out. Pool is so obvious. Just knock the fucking ball in the hole—any idiot can see it. But in three-cushion billiards, where there are no holes, where you have to map out inside your skull the path the balls have to take around the table . . . well, there you have something that takes some brains. You can study three-cushion for a lifetime and learn tricks and variations right up to the end. I've been studying it for fifty years, and I've learned probably fifty new shots in the last five years alone.

Bums play pool, gentlemen play billiards. I noticed it the minute I lit in Chicago. The pool tables were either in the back of the room, or in the basement, so that the pool players wouldn't bother the billiard players. If you walked in a joint needing a shave, they would escort you right to the back, where the rest of the bums were. There was always a sign over the pool tables: "No loud talking. No swearing. No gambling. No massé shots." When one of the players missed a massé shot for some money, he might holler, "Goddam sonofabitching mother-fucker!" and the house man would shout, "Shuddup, you stupid cocksucker! Can't you read?"

They didn't need signs like that for the billiard players, because they weren't the type of people who hollered and cussed; they were allowed to shoot massé shots because they knew what they were doing.

I was a no-good, useless, drunken bum, but I wanted to be a gentleman. The only way open to me was to take up billiards. I didn't think of it that way at the time . . . Christ, I didn't think much about anything. I was just trying to get through each day as best I could. All I knew was that there was something important about billiards, something high class. All the billiard players seemed to have made something of themselves. Playing billiards was like belonging to a private club. Willie Hoppe, Welker Cochran, Jake Schaefer, they were players famous all over the world and they played billiards, not pool. When they saw a pool table they got sick to their stomachs.

When I arrived on the scene, straight billiards—where all you have to do to score a point is make the cueball hit the two other balls—was already in limbo. Jake Schaefer's father had killed it as a spectator sport. That old codger would get the balls trapped against the rail or in a corner and run thousands of points. The only way to stop him from scoring was hit him on the head with a club. When the game was over the ushers would have to slap the spectators in the faces to wake them up.

Something had to be done to make the game tougher. One of the ideas was to make the player hit a rail before hitting the second object ball, or hit the red ball first. Another idea was balkline, where they divided the table up with chalk lines. You couldn't make more than one or two points of straight billiards in any area without driving at least one of the balls into a different area. Things settled down finally to 18.2 balkline, where the lines are drawn eighteen inches from the rails, and you are allowed two points before you have to drive a ball out.

The record book shows that the first big balkline tournament was held in 1903 in Paris. Maurice Vigneaux, a frog, was the winner. I never saw the guy, but I know they called him The Lion because he had a big head of hair. He was the one Hoppe beat in 1906 to win the world title at the age of eighteen. It was a sensation at the time—front-page news, not sports-page news—and from then on you always had to pay money to see Hoppe play.

The first balkline tournament I saw was held in 1921 in the Grand Ballroom of the Congress Hotel in Chicago and was considered a very important event for the whole town. The Chicago Daily News, the Herald Examiner, the Tribune, those papers wrote it up as if the Prince of Wales was playing polo on Michigan Avenue. The spectators had to be very well dressed to get in, and the players wore tuxedos. No kids allowed. No screaming meemies in mothers' arms. The room was plush, with big chandeliers, private boxes all around at the balcony level, a brass rail between the audience and the arena, gold drapes. Just one table. That shit about having more than one table at a time got started much later. I can remember looking up at the ladies in the boxes, watching the game through opera glasses, and wondering if they knew what the hell was going on. Everything was so lavish . . . God, they did things up big then. They packed the people in . . . for an attraction that wouldn't draw flies today. Of course, billiards was a very big sport. In the Loop, at that time, there were at least five hundred billiard tables, and in the middle of the afternoon every one was busy.

The same thing killed balkline that killed straight rail: the players got so good they were boring to watch for the general public. They kept the balls in a little cluster and made cozy shots about an inch long that you couldn't see unless you were kneeling on the table. When a ball had to be driven to the other end of the table, it always came to the cluster as if it was tied to a long rubber band. If Hoppe or Cochran or Schaefer got the balls straddling a chalk line they kept making points until somebody turned out the lights or sprayed them with a hose. Cochran made one run of 684. To wake the audience up after that they had to shoot off a cannon.

Three-cushion—where the cueball has to hit at least three rails and one ball, in any order, before it hits the second ball—is a better spectator sport so it has stayed alive. In three-cushion the shots are big—even the spectators in the cheap seats can see them. Sometimes in order to score you have to drive the cueball forty feet, or twice around the table. The game is so tough it is impossible to really master it. If you make a run of fifteen points in a row you get a standing ovation.

At Bensinger's in Chicago, the billiard tables were on one floor and the pool tables on another. The elevator was an open wrought-iron cage, and I could see the billiard games as I rode up to join the hoodlums on the next floor. After getting hoisted through that billiard atmosphere a thousand times, I decided to get off and see what it was all about. I have never been the same since.

When I stepped off the elevator a broad was right there to take my coat. Thank God I was well dressed that day. She led me to a table covered with beautiful new green cloth . . . Number One Simonis from Belgium, naturally. The best. She spilled out the three balls—clear heart ivory from Zanzibar. Lately we have been running out of elephants, so most billiards today is played with plastic balls, which is not too bad, but nothing like good ivory. The sound ivory balls make when they click together, the way they hesitate before the English takes, the way they hold the spin off the third rail—you just can't beat it. The girl asked me what weight cue I wanted, and when I told her twenty ounces with a twelve-millimeter tip she brought me one that was a dream—two-piece bird's-eye maple, brass joint, inlaid butt, ivory ferrule. I wanted somebody to play with, so she put up a little sign next to the table that said "Three-cushion player wanted." In other words, she treated me as if I was somebody, somebody special, when, as I said, I was nothing but a no-good, useless, drunken fucking bum.

It was quiet as a library in that billiard room. All you could hear was the clicking of the ivory and the bump of the balls against the rubber. If you shouted or swore they were liable to bar you for life. Even if you coughed a little they might ask you to step outside till you got control of yourself. Nothing was allowed that might be the least bit distracting. It almost makes me cry to remember the respect they used to have for billiard players.

A fellow showed up to play me. He was probably a corporation lawyer or a Superior Court judge, for all I know. At least a bail bondsman. He tried to get me to play for a little something, but I ducked that. He beat me without any trouble, but I enjoyed it, enjoyed the atmosphere. When you get beat at something and enjoy it, you've got to like it.

What makes three-cushion a great game is that every move you make is half offense and half defense. Like chess. I don't play chess myself, but that is what chess players tell me. When you study a three-cushion shot you have to estimate the odds of making it, the odds of leaving your opponent a tough shot if you miss, or yourself an easy one if you score. There are damned few really easy shots, but some are easier than others. If you can score one point an inning, on the average—one point each time you get a turn at the table—you are in the world-championship class. In rack pool the top players average about fifteen points an inning, in balkline about thirty-five.

The shots in three-cushion are so tough it is a pleasure when you make one. And it is a pleasure to watch the cueball do what you want it to do—slow down, speed up, curve. When you know what you are doing you can make that cueball act as if it had a mind of its own.

After that afternoon in Bensinger's, I was hooked, and I played three-cushion almost every day from then on. I was hungry for knowledge, and I drove some of the older players nuts with questions. It wasn't long before I was making people sit up and take notice. In 1924 something happened that sealed my fate as billiard bum for life: I won the Chicago Junior Amateur Tournament. There were twenty-four players in it, some of them very good, but all of them fairly young and green. We played twenty-five points of three-cushion in a different place every night—Rogers Park, Evanston, Arlington, all over. My record was 23–1, and for a while there I was the toast of the town. Well, housewives weren't hoisting glasses to me, but I was big in the Loop poolrooms. Up-and-coming young player, and all that.

I was introduced to Willie Hoppe and I almost pissed my pants. You can't believe what an honor it was to shake his hand—it was like meeting Babe Ruth. The fans wanted to see how I would do against various people, so some matches were arranged. I played Alfredo De Oro, who already was pretty old, maybe sixty, and got beat, but I dumped Leon Magnus, who was so old he shook like a leaf. Magnus had won the first three-cushion tournament ever held—in 1878. I'll bet I'm the only guy that has played him, the first champ, and Ceulemans, the current one. In fact, I've played almost all the champs in between, too.

Augie Kieckhefer set up a match for me against Johnny Layton, who was the reigning three-cushion king at the time. He went right through me, but he was a hell of a nice guy and I didn't mind too much. Not on the outside, anyway. Underneath, I promised myself I would learn how he made it look so easy, and why it was when I stepped to the table I never seemed to have anything to shoot at.

A fellow by the name of Dick Adams took me under his wing and was a big help to me. He ran a billiard room on 63rd between University and Woodlawn. According to him I had a perfect billiard stroke and could go all the way to the top if I would quit drinking and learn to control my speed and how to lock up my short-angle shots. What I had to do, he said, was play balkline, and play it, play it, play it. So we played, he and I did, at his place every morning for a year. Every morning it was 200 points of 18.2, and I hated it. It was too small a game for me; I wanted to let my stroke out and see those balls move. Adams taught me the massé, the dead-ball draw, how to kill the speed of the cueball with reverse English off the rail, how to spread the balls so the next shot brought them back together, a hundred things like that. There is no question that learning balkline helped me. There's nothing like it for short shots, speed, and position. Every three-cushion player should practice balkline once in a while. I tell all my students to do it, but few of them do. I can tell by the way they look at me what they are thinking. They are thinking: "What the fuck does that old fart know about it?"

Next time the Junior Amateur came around, in 1925, I was barred. I gambled, the other players said. I hung around with people like Bad Eye and Scarface Foreaker and The Eagle, they said. I was not the clean-cut type of youngster the amateur billiard program was designed to promote, or some such shit, they said. The other players just wanted me out, that's all. I was plenty clean-cut enough when they thought they could beat me. So I learned another important lesson: The better you get the bigger prick you become. You don't really change, but you do in the eyes of your competitors. Everybody loves you as long as they can beat your brains out.

Sure, I hung around with Bad Eye and Scarface. I had to win a match with Scarface, in fact, to get that game with Layton. I've heard people whisper about Scarface, but he is a perfectly fine guy in my book. Last time I saw him was in Sacramento, California. He was running down a sidewalk, going so fast his raincoat was standing straight out behind him. I didn't find out what he had done because I couldn't catch him. All I know is that he was getting lost.

The best three-cushion players in the world were concentrated in Chicago during the 1920's, and I watched them whenever I could. It was in 1923 that the Interstate League started, which really put three-cushion on the map and killed balkline. The Interstate League started out with about a dozen players, each one sponsored by a room in a different town. Every guy had to play every other guy two matches, one at home and one away . . . a double round robin for the championship of the world. They charged $1.10 for front-row seats at the matches, and the rooms were always packed to the rafters. My God, the players . . . the players were the best in the world: Johnny Layton out of Sedalia, Missouri, Tiff Denton playing for Kling and Allen in Kansas City, Augie Kieckhefer representing himself, Bob Cannafax out of Detroit, Gus Copulus playing for the Euclid Arcade in Cleveland, Otto Reiselt for Allinger's in Philadelphia—that gives you an idea of the caliber of play. Hoppe, Cochran, and Schaefer weren't in it. They were opposed to three-cushion. They had balkline locked up—nobody could come close to them—so they fought against three-cushion and didn't take it up until balkline died completely in the 1930's.

There were always at least two of the league players in Chicago, and they kept an open game going in the back room of Kieckhefer's most of the day. Seven points for two dollars. Anybody could play, but you got no spot. There were no spectators allowed . . . this was strictly a players' game. I got in and played with them every chance I could, and it was like going through a meat grinder. If there were, say, six players in the game, you never got more than two or three shots. Somebody would run seven and out, or a four and a three. For a year and a half I played, and one day I broke even. Broke even! I went right out and got drunk, I was so happy.

But it was the best training I could have got. If I became some kind of half-ass billiard player, I owe it to playing in those pot games. It cost me at least ten bucks a day, but it was priceless experience. Cheaper than taking lessons. They didn't mind me, so long as I brought my money and didn't ask for a spot. If I had asked for a spot, they would have said, "Don't let the door hit you in the ass." When they had picked me clean I would race out to Dick Adams's joint and set up shots I had seen played, particularly by Reiselt, who was terrific, and I would talk them over with Dick. "Why did he play it off the white instead of the red? Why did he elevate his cue a little? Why did he bank for this one instead of going cross table? Why did he slow the ball down?" Between the two of us we would figure out the answers. To beat a kiss. To drop the red into the opposite corner. To leave a tough shot. To drive a ball five rails for position.

I didn't quit playing pool entirely, because I had to hustle pool here and there to make a living between jobs, but three-cushion was what I enjoyed doing most. Besides, it is a big help to a hustler to know all games. After beating a guy in rotation it is nice to have him propose a little game of billiards for higher stakes.

I used to make swings through Indiana and Ohio, hustling both pool and billiards, whichever presented itself. One night I was lining up a shot, looking down my cue toward the front door, when I saw a police car pull up in front of the joint. The house man said to me, "Look, kid, I'm going to do you a favor. I called the cops on you. How am I going to make any money off my customers if you get it all? Now beat it out the back way."

He had a point, and I thanked him as I disappeared.

It is much nicer to hustle three-cushion instead of pool, because you rob a more refined type of person. In three-cushion, the worst that can happen is to have the guy ask you if you will take a check. But you beat a guy out of a few bucks in a pool game and he might pick up the cueball and knock your teeth out.

I have never taken a ball in the teeth, but I have taken checks. I was working for Cliquot Club as a salesman. One morning after the daily sales meeting, the pep talk—"Get out there and sell . . ." and so on—I ducked into 18 East Randolph Street. It was winter, the air was full of those white flies, the streets were a mess of dirty slush. I wanted to play billiards, I didn't want to get out there and sell. I got a set of balls and was knocking them here and there when a very solid citizen type asked me if I wanted to indulge in a little game.

"Why not?" I said. "I have to wait here until my secretary calls, anyway."

The guy had a big stickpin in his tie with a headlight on it, and another flasher on his ring. "Care to make it interesting?" he said while he chalked his cue.

"Anything you say, pal." I had plenty of money. I was doing well enough hustling so that my commissions from Cliquot Club were going right in the bank.

We decided on ten points for two dollars. After the first few shots I saw that the guy couldn't even *spell* billiards. We played six games and he never got more than five points.

When we quit he went up to the desk and paid the time with a bill he peeled off a roll he could hardly get his fingers around. Then to me he said, "I trust you will accept a check?"

"Holy shit," I said, "you got a roll you couldn't flush down a toilet and you want to give me a check?"

"I assure you the check is good. Furthermore, I enjoyed playing with you and I would like to meet you here next Friday at the same time for another session, and the Friday after that."

Talk about the soft con! But there was something solid about him. I took a chance.

The check was on the LaSalle Trust and Savings at LaSalle and Monroe, where I happened to know a teller by the name of Shorty Hackman. I busted over there through the slush.

"Say, Shorty, how good is this check?"

"Just a minute and I'll tell you if it is any good at all." He looked something up. "The check is good."

"Shorty, how good is it?"

"Danny, my friend, you could sign a long string of zeros on the end of it."

At 9:30 next Friday morning I came out of the sales meeting at Cliquot Club. It was a beautiful day—no slush, no white flies. A good day to call on my accounts and try to work up some new business. But it was the appointed hour, so I ducked into Kieckhefer's. There were fifty-five tables on one floor . . . forty billiards in front and fifteen pockets in the back. At that time of day there was nothing doing but one snooker game way in the corner. I hung around the top of the stairs, and sure enough, here came my opponent through the door. I raced to the back of the room and slumped into a chair and pretended to be watching the snooker game. He looked around, spotted me, walked back to where I was sitting, and tapped me on the shoulder.

"Well, hello!" I said.

"Shall we play?" he said.

We played every Friday for six weeks. He never won a game and his checks never bounced. I could count on twelve bucks a week like clockwork. Plenty of my so-called friends tried to get him away from me, but he wasn't interested. He had taken a liking to me, or some damned thing. I was supposed to be a killer, but I got to feeling a little sorry for this particular guy. One day I showed up half drunk after being out all night. As we were lagging for the break I turned to him and said, "Listen, why don't you smarten up? You won't beat me in a thousand years."

What he said to me made me feel about an inch tall. He said, "I know that, Dan, but don't you think I'm improving?"

A couple of Fridays later he didn't show up. I figured he was sick, and I half expected him to phone in or send a note. When he didn't show the next week either, or the week after, I went over to see Shorty at the bank.

"Hey, what happened to my meal ticket?"

Shorty looked in a few filing cabinets. "Danny, he's moved his account to Boston. He's gone."

"Who the hell was he, anyway?"

"You didn't know? He's the vice president of the Metropolitan Life Insurance Company."

"The vice president?"

"That's right. One of the richest legitimate guys in the country. He probably paid you by check so he could deduct you from his income tax or put you on his expense account."

I've often wondered how he handled that, how he accounted for all those "Pay to the order of Danny McGoorty . . . $12.00." Maybe he put me down as a consulting engineer. Or a ballet teacher.

5

Horses

I started playing the horses early, when I was on my way with two Irish kids to a pool hall at 55th and Ellis. We got caught in a rainstorm on Cottage Grove across from Washington Park, and we ducked into a doorway of what turned out to be a bookie joint, complete with walls covered with tip sheets and results. "They're off at Narragansett," a voice was saying over a loudspeaker. We didn't know what it was all about at first, but when it dawned on us we stepped inside, even though we only had a dollar between us.

They had phone lines open to Suffolk Downs, Louisville, New Orleans, even Havana. A guy was announcing the race from a ticker tape, giving phony descriptions . . . re-creations. "It's Birdshit on the rail . . ." and so forth.

The place was full of people, so nobody paid any attention to a few punk kids. I picked up a racing form from a counter and started looking it over as if I knew how to read it. All of a sudden I saw a nag by the name of Lucky Dan. "I have a cinch," I said, "an absolute cinch. Let's run that buck of ours into something big." I whipped out my twenty cents and slapped it down, but it was like pulling teeth to get my one pal to put up his forty-five cents and the other his thirty-five.

With a dollar in change I went up to a window and shoved it under the grill. "Put it all on Lucky Dan," I said.

The guy didn't bat an eye. "How do you want it?" he said.

"What do you mean, 'How do I want it'?" I didn't know how the fuck I wanted it.

"Well, I mean do you want it on the snout, or what?"

"Yeah, that's it. On the snout."

He gave me a ticket and we sat back and waited. Pretty soon they were announcing the race. "At the quarter it is Mazzola and Appleknocker . . . At the half it is Whozit . . ." No mention of Lucky Dan at all, and I am catching daggers from the two Irishmen. "They are turning into the stretch . . . into the straightaway . . . they are in a bunch at the wire . . . it is a blanket finish." Then came the first mention of our horse. "The winner is Lucky Dan." That goddam horse paid $68.40! Jesus Christ Almighty. We were all so happy I talked them into giving me half the winnings.

That night my aunts heard the heavy jingle in my pockets and noticed my devil-may-care attitude. They asked me where I got the money and said that they would be able to tell if I was lying. So I confessed to having won it in a crap game and promised never to do it again. That satisfied them. Dice and cards, for some reason, didn't upset them as much as horses.

For a while my friends asked me to pick winners for them. I thought I had a special touch myself, but my reputation didn't last very long.

I want to get one thing across about horse racing, which is something I know quite a bit about. Well, actually, I know very little about it. All I know is that picking winners is a matter of sheer, dumb luck. I went back to that book every day for a month until I could read the racing form pretty good . . . how much the horse carries, what he did last year, how he finished a week ago Tuesday. Racing forms in those days were much more detailed than they are now because there weren't as many horses to cover. You could find out all kinds of facts. I found out that Lucky Dan hadn't been in the money for four years and that he was ten years old. That shows how lucky you have to be.

Winning a bet on a horse at an early age is one of the worst things that can happen to you. It was an accident that I didn't get bit by the bug worse than I did, for which I can thank Augie Kieckhefer. He made me forget about horse racing altogether for a number of years. Augie owned not only the big room in the Loop but a big billiard chalk business that his father left him, and was worth hundreds of thousands of dollars. He kept two phones at his desk so he could call his book and his book could call him. He lost the whole works, every fucking nickel his father left him, over those horses.

A few years later I got stung again. I was picking winners like mad, but losing money because I didn't know how to bet, didn't know how to manage my taw. Once I picked four winners out of eight races and lost nine hundred dollars. So I quit that sport again. It is a bad deal because you don't have any personal control over what is happening. You never know when the nags are doped or the jockeys have something cooked up.

Jockeys can do all sorts of things. Two or three can gang up on the favorite and box him in, make sure he doesn't win. Hell, I've had jockeys stand up in the stirrups in the stretch and haul back on the reins just to beat me out of the money. Before cameras came in it was hard to catch these things, hard to prove anything. Now they keep a camera on everybody from the front, back, side, everywhere, and they have to keep pretty much in line. One thing they still do is let some other jockey have it right in the teeth with a whip, which sort of throws the man off stride.

But it is hard to resist going to the track when there is nothing doing at a billiard room. You have got to have something working for you at all times, otherwise you stand no chance of making any kind of a score. So I keep finding myself at horse races with guys who are worse idiots than I am. As long as I keep thinking of Augie, though, I am all right.

6

Two
Orgies

One

There was a bohunk girl used to hang around at the dances at the Midway Gardens. Not what you would call pretty, but well built, as I noticed when I found out she was a virgin. A lot of guys had tried, but nobody had been on base. Well, I said to myself, I am going to try my luck.

I cut in on her about halfway through the eighth dance. I had danced with her a time or two on other nights, so we weren't complete strangers. She gave me a nice hello, and when I put a little pressure on her shoulder blades she brought her cheek right up to mine. Pelvis to pelvis we danced. She made no move to back away even when I dropped my hand down around her keester.

People cut in on each other a lot during the dances, but I finished every one with her, and there were sixteen.

"Who is taking you home?" I asked her at the end.

"You are," she said. "I live at 98th and Exchange."

"Holy Christ," I said, "that's miles. Look, I know a place at 48th and Prairie. Friends of mine. Let's go there."

She didn't squawk at all. It was duck soup, I thought. I was in like a burglar. What was so tough about this broad? I had money, so outside I herded her into a taxi and gave my pals a big wink and the high sign as we pulled away.

In the cab we did some tongue sucking, and I got my hand . . . well, not actually in her box, but damned close to it. You've got to remember that in those days the broads wore coats and dresses and slips and petticoats and bloomers and garter belts and slings and underpants and stepins and Christ, I don't know what all. To get on base . . . to even *find* the base . . . you had to be practically a *prospector*.

The place I took her to was a speakeasy . . . a bootlegging joint . . . that rented out trick rooms. It was pitch dark outside, and there was no sign of any kind.

"What is this?" she said.

"This is the place we are going to."

"Oh," she said. "Okay."

She was giving me no resistance at all.

I gave the door the old dump-diddy-dump-dump, dump-dump, and an iron slot shot back just like in the Untouchables. A pair of eyes looked us over and a voice said, "Danny!" It was Daisy, the manager. Now this joint was just like a regular home. No big bar or anything. You just took your date into one of the bedrooms and Daisy would get you anything you wanted from the kitchen. I made the "take it slow" sign to her behind the bo-hunk's back, so Daisy let us sit in the parlor and served some Panther Piss with home brew beer for a chaser. Incidentally, Panther Piss was really the name of a line of moonshine. The name was right on the label, which had a drawing of a panther pissing. It was quite a novelty item. People used to collect those labels, but I haven't seen one for thirty years.

After half an hour or so Daisy came in and said, "Listen, I

don't want to rush you, but I got just one room left and it ain't gonna last forever. If you want it you better speak up."

I looked over at the bohunk broad and said, "By the way, do we want that room?"

"Whatever you say, Danny."

She wasn't talking like a virgin, but it was too late in the day to start caring about that.

"Okay, Daisy," I said, "we'll take it. Send us in a couple of bottles of Piss and half a pint of Jackass."

The Panther Piss was two dollars a pint, and the room was three bucks for the night. There were better bargains, but this was a high-class joint.

After Daisy left the tray and said good night, my broad did a little striptease, taking off this and taking off that, all the while shooting me little smiles. Usually you had to encourage them, but not this broad . . . she was ready. When she got down to her brassiere and panties she giggled and jumped in the bed, pulling the sheets up to her nose and waiting for me to make the next move.

So I started a little striptease. I took a few things off, every once in a while leaning down to give her a slobber. Why hurry? I wanted her to get the idea that she was in the hands of a master. I sat on the edge of the bed and took off one shoe and then the other, throwing them aside with a little toss of my head. Man, I was nonchalant, and all the while with a stiff in my shorts you could have hung a bucket of sand on. She wasn't saying "Hurry up," or anything like that, but with her eyes she was giving me the feeling that she was getting very impatient.

It was about two in the morning when I finally got under the sheets with her. We had a few last drinks, then I turned off the light. She bellied right up to me. I reached around and unhooked her brassiere . . . I had no trouble with that at all. I put my hands all over, then hooked my thumbs over her panties and started to pull them down . . .

"No," she said.

"Huh?"

"No."

"Don't take off the pants?"

"No. Not yet."

"Jesus Christ," I said, "when, then?"

"Well, not right now."

Before I could squawk she started giving me slobbers right and left and hugging me and jamming herself against me. Then she started getting her gun off! Just by grinding her pelvis against me! Quick as I could I tried to take her pants down but it was no dice. She locked her legs in a scissors and there was no way.

I got to shorten this story up. It's too painful. I spent the whole night wrestling with that broad, trying to get those goddam pants off. With our arms and legs wrapped around each other, we would fall onto the floor, and we would bump and roll, going from one side of the room to the other, under the bed, into the closet, back up on the bed. I don't know what people in the other rooms thought, or even people walking by outside.

More than once I rolled over on my back and put my hands over my face and said, "Oh, Jesus, I can't take any more of this . . . this is killing me." My John Henry would start to sag, but when she felt that happening she would grab me, grab me, don't you understand? She couldn't stand the thought of my willie going limp. She would throw herself on me and suck my tongue and put her hands all over and start getting her gun off again and I would think, oh, she is ready now, she is out of control, and I would hook my thumbs over those panties and strain, and we would go through the whole thing again—on the floor, into the corner, under the bed, into the closet . . . all night and all morning until I was a nervous wreck and completely worn out and had to give up.

At noon I was sicker than a dog and she was still a virgin. I shouted at her to get dressed, and she did, sort of whimpering, afraid I was going to throttle her, I suppose, and maybe I should have. She was crazy to put me through that. Anybody else would have killed her. I was sick, sick for a week. It is terrible to get worked up like that over and over and not be able to get rid of the stuff—it gets absorbed back into your system and raises hell with you—I know what I am talking about. I put her on a streetcar at one-thirty in the afternoon without even giving her a chance to comb her hair or wipe off her smeared make-up. Listen, she was lucky.

I saw her many times at dances after that but I never went anywhere near her. About a year later she married Rocky Indiana, a small-time prize fighter that sometimes hung around. One day I met him on the street alone and I said to him, "Rocky, you've got to tell me something. Don't shit me, please. This is something I've got to know. Was your wife a virgin when you got married?"

He didn't take offense at all. "Yes, she was, Danny," he said, "and I wouldn't shit you about a thing like that."

"I don't think you would. Thanks a lot."

I felt better. If some other asshole had gotten on base after all the work I had put in, I think I would have gone off the Tribune Tower.

Two

By the time I am twenty-six years old I am through busting virgins. Too much work! I am leaving that to the younger guys. One night I am sitting in the kitchen of a speakeasy having a few drinks with Jimmy Carver, a good friend of mine, when in walks a clown we both know by the name of Butterfield. Now this Butterfield is a skinny, homely sonofabitch with straight red hair that won't stay combed and a complexion like a fart through a keg of nails. But he has a tomato with him that is out of this fucking world! Where he got her, how he got her, is a big mystery, but she is a dream—a solidly packed, absolutely perfect shape inside a tailored white suit, with long hair hanging down and eyes that would shine in the dark. Here is probably the best-looking broad I have ever seen in my whole life, walking around with an idiot who stinks on ice. Butterfield gives us a look as much as to say, "Look what I've got," and, by God, he had something.

"I want you to meet a friend of mine, McGoor," he says. A lot of people called me "McGoor" for short. That, or "prick." "This is Cora Blackburn."

"Well, hello," I say.

I feed a few nickels into the player piano to get a little dance music, and then I ask Butterfield if he has ever seen Jimmy Carver's car. Carver has the family Locomobile with him this night, and it is a fantastic thing, all aluminum, made for a movie back in 1922. His folks have money and picked it up at an auction. It is a touring car, long as a whore's dream, with all sorts of fancy attachments, like a rear window wiper and three horns. Butterfield has heard about it but has never seen it, and as soon as he and Carver are outside I have Cora on the dance floor. I test her, see how far I can drop my hand down her back and so on, and she stands right up to me and doesn't flinch. She feels awful good, and her eyes look right through to the back of my head. Pretty soon I ask where she lives. She gives me an address on Englewood.

"Do you live alone, or what?" Kind of a dumb question, because she is only about eighteen years old.

"No," she says, "I live with my mother, but she is away for a couple of weeks in Buffalo."

"You are living alone in a thirteen-room house?"

"How did you know it has thirteen rooms?"

"Because all the houses on that part of Englewood have thirteen rooms." I learned that driving cab. "Look, what the hell are we drinking two-dollar Panther Piss in this joint for? Let's go over to your place. I know a very good bootlegger in that neighborhood. Come on, we'll get another girl or two and have a little party."

She thinks this is a fine idea, so we all pile in the Locomobile and take off, even though Butterfield is getting a little nervous. We stop at a speakeasy and I pop inside. There is only one broad in there that I know. I say to her, "Don't buy any more grog in this joint. I've got a real good guy out in the Locomobile for you and we have a hell of a deal cooked up." By a real good guy I mean Carver, not that asshole Butterfield, who I am hoping will get the message and get lost . . . but no, he sticks to us like glue.

This house of Cora's is a very nice place. Big. All the furniture looks heavy. Polished woodwork. Rugs. It is dark when we get there, but we soon change that. We turn on all the lights and start knocking off the bottles in the liquor cabinet one after another. I have Cora under my wing and Butterfield starts hollering about it, but we just keep pouring the booze down him. Carver and the other broad are getting along fine, so Butterfield should have got the idea that he is just excess baggage.

Next thing I know it is morning and Butterfield has me by the shoulder and is shaking the shit out of me. I have such a hangover I have trouble coming into focus, but pretty soon I see that I am in bed with Cora in the master bedroom. She is stark naked and I am in her mother's red kimono. "McGoorty, you sonofabitch," Butterfield is saying, "you've taken my girl away from me, you dirty, rotten bastard . . ."

At this Cora pushes herself up on one elbow, and what a set of tits she has! "*Your* girl," she says. "Where did you get the idea that I was *your* girl?"

Butterfield staggers out and starts hitting the bottle again. Carver comes down from the third floor with his squaw and we go into the kitchen to have a little breakfast and a few drinks. Well, after a few days of this we run out of booze. We start sending out for it. When we run out of money I start writing notes for Carver to take to all the bootleggers: "Please give bearer four bottles and oblige. I'll take care of this next Tuesday. Danny McGoorty." By God if this didn't work a few times.

That house gradually begins to look like the city dump. All the wastebaskets are full of empty bottles, and so are some orange crates somebody dragged up from the basement. The kitchen is a big garbage pile.

At the end of a week the five of us are still there, although Butterfield is in such a stupor that we have to kick him every once in a while to see if he's still alive. We are out of food and money and credit, but I manage to think of a way to keep the party going a little while longer. I know where some of the guys meet before going to the dances—they meet at Charley Brush's pool hall, or Dick Adams's, or the Woodlawn Recreation. They fight the mirrors there for an hour or so before going to the hop. So I call them on the phone and say, "Listen, if you get a broad tonight, don't go to a speakeasy or a hotel. Come over to so-and-so Englewood Avenue. If you want to turn a trick you won't have to worry about signing a register someplace. The admission is a bottle."

Well, Jesus Christ, you talk about a hoormaster! That night the house is crawling with people. I am shagging them out of one bedroom as fast as I am shagging them into another, while all the time Cora is stockpiling Panther Piss of all descriptions.

This goes on for another week, but it is all pretty hazy. I remember that Carver's girl got sick for awhile, and whenever she moaned for a glass of water we brought her a shot of whiskey. Then we got a telegram from Cora's mother: "Be home tomorrow night, darling, hope you missed me," or some shit along those lines.

"The mother is coming?" says Carver. "Who?" says somebody else. "Cora's mother." "Cora's mother is coming here?" "Cora who? Who's Cora?" "You mean Cora's mother is coming here?" That kind of conversation. We are all so blind you have to repeat everything a dozen times to make any headway at all.

Right away everybody gets lost except Cora and me. They just disappear, and we are left with the mess. We have one day to clean up the joint, and as I walk around looking things over I sober up pretty fucking fast. There are cigarette burns on the grand piano three inches long. And on the rugs. There are glasses and bottles standing everywhere, half of them tipped over. There are vests and stockings that people have forgotten. There are used condoms on the love seats and settees and behind sofa pillows and draped over pictures on the walls. There are even Kotexes here and there—we had some Red Riders of Bloody Gulch. The sheets on the beds—God, I have never seen anything like it. There is no use turning them over because they are just as ruined on one side as the other. Some maidens were had, that's for sure. The kitchen is so stacked up you can hardly get into it.

Now here is something that stands out as plain as day. Cora and I are lying on the bed in the master bedroom, which is behind some sliding doors just off the dining room. I am in the mother's kimono, which I never took off since the night I arrived. "We've got to get some help to clean this place up," I am saying to her. "I don't want to run out on you, I want to help you. Here's what I'm gonna do. I'm gonna call around to the rooms and see if I can round up a gang of guys that will come over here and do some work, because this joint looks like a whorehouse—shit, worse than a whorehouse. If it looked like a whorehouse it wouldn't be so bad . . ."

WHOOSH! The sliding doors fly open and who is standing there? The mother! Cora's mother! Standing there with her hands up and her chin on her belt buckle . . . she can't believe her eyes. Oh, man, then the screaming started. "My baby! My daughter! My baby daughter!" And to me: "You fiend! You beast! You disgusting, filthy maniac!" I don't remember what all she shouted, but it was very high-class stuff. No profanity. She was hotter than hell, but she didn't cuss at me.

I start making my move. I throw off the kimono . . .

"My kimono!" the mother screams. "My best kimono! Oh, no!"

I am looking for my shorts—never mind the shorts—I put on my pants and go for my shoes—no time for socks . . .

"Don't worry," Cora says.

"Don't worry," I say. "Are you crazy?"

All the while the mother is screaming bloody murder and waving her fists at me. I finally find two left shoes and get into them and I throw on a raincoat and I sail out a back door with no shirt or socks—just shoes, pants, and a raincoat. Through the garden I go and over a six-foot fence into the alley. All the streets in Chicago have alleys.

When I hit 63rd Street I finally get lucky—a rattler is coming by, and I jump aboard. I am lucky, too, that the old dame didn't call the cops before she busted in on us.

The conductor looks at me as if I am something that came floating out of a sewer. What a mess: solid red eyes, hair like a bird's nest, a two-day beard, two left shoes . . . and I don't have any money, not a cent—nothing. Not even a wrist watch or a scrap of identification.

"Listen," I say to the conductor, "give me a break. I left my money in my other pants. I had a little trouble . . ."

"You sure as hell must have . . ."

"Give me a lift, please . . . I've got to get home. It's an emergency . . . I'll mail you the token on Tuesday."

He looks at me for a long time, shaking his head like he can't believe it, then he gives in. "Okay," he says with a wave of his hand, "go on in and siddown. But you sure take the fucking cake."

"Jesus Christ, thanks a lot, mister."

As I go by him he catches me by the shoulder. "I suppose you want a *transfer*."

"No, I don't want a *transfer*."

I make it to a room I am renting and flop on the bed until I can pull myself together. I am too nervous to stay there, so I get up, take a shower, shave, and put on some clean clothes. I go down to Dick Adams's room wondering if there is a warrant out for my arrest. I sit at the back of the room for awhile trying to get interested in two old men playing a game of snooker for three cents on the pink ball and nineteen cents on the black. When the phone rings I jump a foot.

"I'm not here!" I hiss at Adams, waving my arms. "I'm never here . . . I don't come in here . . . you never heard of me . . ."

"Yeah, he's here," Adams says into the phone, "hang on a minute." To me he says, "She knows you're here, Danny. Somebody named Cora."

Now I know goddam well I didn't give her the number of this room. Unless I was drunk.

"Cora! Why did you call me here? Don't you think I am in enough trouble?"

"My mother is not going to talk to you that way," she says.

"Look, let's just forget it for awhile."

"We are not going to forget anything, honey baby. I ran away from home. I'm just not going to listen to anybody talk about you like that. I'm at the Hayes Hotel. Room 511. Knock three times."

There was only one thing I could do. I knocked three times. She opened the door and pasted a big slobber on me and a minute later we were in bed. Do you know we didn't leave that room for a week? We stayed right there drinking a very high grade of alky and bumping the pelvis bones together. She had cashed a check for sixty dollars and had credit at the desk, so we had no money problems. I was even buying whiskey off the bellboy, and when you buy it that way it is high. The Hayes Hotel was a very nice place; all the visiting baseball teams stayed there. So we didn't suffer any. Had the best meals in the house sent up. Even had a few friends over. Everything went on the bill.

In the mornings the maid knocked on the door. "Want your room made up today?"

I was not supposed to be in there—Cora was paying a single rate—so I coached her on what to say. "I'm not feeling well today, maid. Just leave the towels by the door and I'll pick them up later."

That worked until Friday. There was a knock on the door. "Just leave the towels there, maid," Cora said.

"It's your mother, dear."

Holy Christ, it was the goddam *mother* again! When I heard that voice I damned near shit. We were on the fifth floor, with no fire escape. I told Cora to keep quiet, to not say another word. The mother would have to go away sooner or later to get the manager or the house dick, which would give me a chance to make a break for it.

I could hardly believe it, but there I was, going for my shoes and pants again—never mind the shorts and socks. My God, I thought to myself, I must be dreaming.

The mother kept knocking and hollering, but Cora and I kept our traps shut until she finally went away. I slowly opened the door and looked both ways. The hall was empty.

"Good-by!" I said to Cora, who gave me a big slobber on the ear as I squeezed past her.

I headed down the corridor toward the elevator and Jesus Christ if the mother didn't pop into view. She had rung for the elevator and was coming back to keep an eye on our door. When she saw me she exploded. "You! You fiend! You maniac! What have you done to my baby daughter? I'll have you put in jail for life . . ."

The elevator doors opened behind her, and as she made a lunge for me with her claws I sidestepped around her so fast she might as well have been nailed to the floor. "Excuse me, lady," I said.

The elevator operator is a real old geezer who is not too fast on the uptake. "Down," I said to him. "Come on, *down*, and step on it. Can't you hear? Goddammit, *down*!"

The mother was racing toward us shouting, "Wait! Stop!"

"I think I see somebody else coming," the old guy said.

"You old cocksucker," I said, "take this sonofabitch down . . ." I grabbed the door out of his hand and slammed it shut just in time. I pushed the lever and left the mother behind trying to pry the wall open with her fingernails.

The elevator was so slow I couldn't stand it, and the operator was looking like he was going to have a shit hemorrhage, so I jumped off on the third floor and flew down a flight of stairs that took me out on University without having to go by the main desk.

I was scared to death, and for the next two weeks I stayed off the street and out of pool halls. I expected the cops to break into my room at any minute, but they never did. Do you know why? Because Cora told her mother that if anything happened to me she would become a whore. But the mother kept her locked up for weeks, and then sent her to school in various foreign countries. In the next few years we saw each other a few times. We never had another around-the-clock drunken marathon, but we did a good bit of organ grinding.

Oh, I'll never forget Cora. She was a dream.

7

Cops
and
Robbers

In Chicago in the twenties it was hard to tell the cops from the robbers. The mob ran the whorehouses, the speakeasies, and the gambling joints, while the cops protected them for a piece of the action. If an outsider came to town and opened something up on his own, there was practically a race to see if the mob could bomb him out before the cops threw him in jail. As far as I could see, the town would have been no different if the gangsters had all changed clothes with the cops.

This is no bullshit. One night when I was driving cab, I pulled up in front of a whorehouse called the Midnight Frolics and saw Chief of Detectives John Skagey slapping the piss out of Johnny Torrio, who was a very big mobster indeed. It was Torrio, in fact, who brought Capone in from New York. But there he was, getting slapped all around by a cop and not saying much about it. He must have missed a payment or something.

I shouldn't really say "the mob," because before Capone got

control of everything there were actually seven mobs, and the competition was fierce. There were murders right and left. Murder was so common it wasn't even news. Nobody ever got arrested, which gives an idea of how things were arranged.*

I could have gotten into alcohol or white slavery or dope—anything I wanted. I knew a lot of people and I was pretty well liked. I was a good billiard player, so that made me stick out a little. Some of the big hoods came into the rooms once in a while to bet on me and kid around with me. They tried to give me jobs—two hundred, four hundred bucks a week—Christ, they were hard to turn down. They usually wanted me to be a driver, a wheel-man, running alky here and there. After all, I was Transportation Dan. A wheel-man was considered higher than a punk, at least, who would do anything for a buck, but not as high as a triggerman. The guy with the sawed-off is naturally the boss. Running alky, it was the triggerman's job to protect that load of grog.

The way they used to pack that alky into those cars! The floorboards came off and the bottom of the car was hollowed out. The alky was packed in there so solid it looked like the wall of a drugstore. A car loaded like that was worth a fortune, so they needed drivers they could trust. I could be trusted on a deal like that, I will say that for myself. I have never stolen a fucking nickel in my life. Those hoods knew that if I said I would drive a load of grog to Gary I wouldn't go to North Platte instead. But I didn't like the odds. There was too much shooting and rough stuff going on, and whenever there was a roust or a bust it was always the small fry who were thrown in the bucket. So I stayed clear of it.

---

*According to Ovid Demaris in *Captive City* (Lyle Stuart, 1969), there were 629 unsolved gang killings within the city limits of Chicago between 1920 and 1931, as well as more than 5,000 homicides. The same book quotes a Treasury Department official's estimate that in 1950 forty police captains in Chicago were worth more than a million dollars each. —RB

I think the reason my aunts put up with me as long as they did—with my gambling and drinking and carousing—was that I stayed out of the rackets. They were worried to death about it, and that probably helped me resist the easy money, because I knew that if I ever showed up wearing a silk suit with a black shirt and a white tie they both would have died of conniption fits. They probably would have anyway if they had known how close I was to it, that I knew personally people like Greasy Thumb Guzik, the O'Donnell brothers, Danny Stanton, Mitters Foley, Joe Saltis, Dingbat Oberta . . . Christ, I could name them all.

Dingbat Oberta . . . he was Big Tim Murphy's chauffeur. When Big Tim got back after a stint in the pen he found Dingbat wearing his pajamas, but before he could do anything about it he answered the front doorbell one day and was met by the usual hail of lead. I don't know how many slugs they picked out of him. I didn't need my aunts to tell me to stay away from that stuff.

Come to think of it, I did do a little bootlegging for awhile, but only after it got so widespread the mob couldn't keep up with it. At first I made bathtub gin just for my own consumption—and I really consumed—but later I made enough to sell to friends of mine. Hank Noonan and I set up a brewery and distillery in a room we rented in the Miramar Hotel, 6268 Woodlawn Avenue, Chicago, Illinois. I should have had my head examined to go in with a strange nut like Noonan, but I didn't know just how nuts he was. Because of him I came within a whisker of getting put in the bucket forever.

Our beat was the dances. We would show up wearing long overcoats with nineteen inside pockets, each one big enough for a fourteen-ounce bottle, or more often an eleven-ounce "flat." A guy who is half loaded and thirsty isn't going to stop to count ounces. Noonan worked night and day at it, like a fanatic, but I always knocked off to have a good time as soon as I had some money in my pocket. Usually we didn't have to go around hustling it—our customers came to us.

I had a guy knock on the door one night and holler, "Open up!"

"Who is it?" I said.

"Open up or I'll break the door down."

So I had to dump five gallons of fresh grog at five dollars a gallon down the flusher. Naturally it wasn't the cops. It was just one of my so-called friends, Tommy McGloughlin, having a little fun.

I'll tell you the trouble with my partner Noonan. Broads. Every broad he met he tried to get up in our room and take her pants off. He got very mean when he ran into any resistance.

I made an awful good move one night. I was going back to the room and in front of the hotel I saw squad cars and flashing red lights and heard loud talking. I did an about-face and headed in the opposite direction, and it was a good thing I did. That crazy Noonan had taken a girl up to the room and raped her, and broke her leg, and paralyzed her. She had put up a fight. "No woman turns me down," he said. I heard him say it many times. I heard him say it to broads who . . . well, some guys don't care what they screw.

They took him to jail and put him under a $25,000 bond. Next day they wheeled the girl in to see the judge and he raised it to $100,000. Now Noonan's old man had money and tried to get Clarence Darrow to defend him, but Darrow was tied up with the Loeb-Leopold case, which, incidentally, I got into one day for about forty-five minutes. You had to know somebody to get in for even that long, because it was a very popular attraction. Anyway, old man Noonan finally settled for W. W. "Ropes" O'Brien, who got his nickname because he was supposed to know the ropes behind the scenes. The story on him was that he was always making deals with the state. If he was defending two different guys on murder raps, he would say to the state: "Let's make a deal. You take one, I'll take one." If you got caught in a caper and wound up with "Ropes" O'Brien, you might as well play Russian roulette. He might get you off but you would never know how and it would be strictly luck. I knew him well. I used to drink with him. He offered to poke me in the nose many times.

Hank's dad paid "Ropes" a retainer of $10,000, but when he got to know him he dropped him and hired another well-known lawyer named Bob Cantwell, whose retainer was $25,000. That was smart, because Cantwell got him off with a life sentence in the first trial, which was thrown out on a technicality, and ten years in the second one.

My name came up one day. The D.A. had Hank in the witness chair. "Did you live in that room alone?"

"No," Hank said, "I lived there with another guy."

I am sitting in the audience scared out of my wits. Shamrock Eakin leans over to me and says, "You little prick, they are going to get you now. You've been out of jail long enough."

Everybody around us says "Shh! Shh!" But they know he is just rousting me.

"Who was the other guy?" the D.A. asks Hank.

"Danny McGoorty," Hank says in a loud, clear voice.

Shamrock leans over to me again. "If I were you," he whispers, "I would take it on the Arthur Duffy. Heel and toe it out of here."

He wanted me to get lost, but how could I stand up in the middle of the courtroom and walk out? I had to sit tight.

For some reason, the D.A. didn't get interested in Danny McGoorty. He didn't follow it up . . . why, I don't know.

Hank didn't serve the whole ten years. He was out in a little over six. But he was dingy after that . . . real dingy. The guards must have worked him over pretty good.

I had a couple of other close shaves in the twenties. I was in a car with a bunch of drunks one night with the cops chasing us all over the Loop. We had been driving on the sidewalk and on the wrong side of the street, sending cars and people up the sides of buildings. When we heard the siren the guy driving our car stepped on it. He must have been a professional wheel-man, because at about the third turn he put the cop car right into a fireplug. The coppers jumped out and opened up with their shotguns. Only one of us got hit—me, naturally. I caught buckshot all over my back—I still have the scars. It wasn't bad, though; I didn't even go to a doctor. Some guy at a poolroom picked the pellets out with a penknife. The hell of it was that I wasn't guilty of anything. All I was doing was riding in a car shitting my pants.

Another time I was sitting in Nelson's Cafeteria with a good friend of mine named Gordon Thexton, whose main mission in life was to get me in trouble. We were drunk. At the next table were two guys from out of town, which was obvious because of the ulsters they were wearing. Coats with huge collars like they had on meant that they had to be from Philly, New York, or Boston. Baltimore, at least. I found out later that they were from Philly. Capone had sent for them to work as bouncers at the Four Deuces. They were two of the meanest hoods in town, but they looked stupid.

"I'll bet you got shit in your blood," Gordy says to me.

"What do you want me to do now?"

"See those two guys? One is getting ready to eat a steak. Grab it and slide it across the floor."

"Fuck you," I say. "Do it yourself. Why should I do a thing like that?"

"Because they are visiting our city. Somebody should introduce them to Chicago. If you won't do it, I will."

"You will like hell . . . you are too chickenshit."

"Well," he says, "if you aren't chickenshit, why don't you do it? Let's have some fun with these guys."

So I do it. Gordy always works it around so I end up doing everything. I get up and walk over to the other table.

"Excuse me, sir," I say to this one hood. I slip my hand under his steak, and with my other hand I kind of brush the onions and mushrooms off it. "Let me show you what can be done with a steak like this." I turn around and lean over and with a sort of backhand flip I spin that fucking steak about a hundred feet across the tile floor. If you've ever been in Nelson's you know that it is a real long sonofabitch.

When I look back to see the expression on the guy's face, the cocksucker comes out of his hip pocket with a sap and hits me right across the bridge of the nose. Knocks my nose clear over to the side of my face. I hit the deck, out like a light. The hood is about to let me have it again in the face, which probably would have killed me, but Dinny Cooney, who is Democratic committeeman in that ward, sees the action and holds up his hand. He must be higher up with Capone than the two hoods, because they put their saps away and take a walk. Cooney knows me, knows that I am just a drunken asshole that means no harm.

Jesus Christ, my nose! It is swollen up for months! A doctor taped it to a wooden stick so it would grow back more or less straight. Gordon Thexton enjoyed the whole thing very much. Every time he saw me with my nose in a splint he broke up.

Getting my snout busted hurt, but not as much as driving my thumb-bone into my wrist. It happened when I squared off against Tommy Cleary on the ice outside the Trianon Ballroom. He wouldn't take off his gloves. With leather gloves on you can cut a guy to ribbons.

"Take off your gloves," I said.

"Fuck you," he said.

"Okay, you bastard," I said, and I let him have it, and with my first punch I laid his forehead open. I swung again, but I slipped on the ice and caught him behind the ear in a way that drove my thumb back into my wrist. That put both of us out of action. The fight was over. All the girls were crying. I was declared the winner, but my hand was hurting so much I could hardly stand it. The bone of my thumb was down inside my hand someplace. Nobody had a knife or a scissors, but a cab driver came along who had a pliers. He grabbed my thumb with the pliers and yanked it back into position. I was so numb I hardly felt a thing. All I could feel was a throbbing—boom, boom, boom. I never did go to a doctor and have it reset, although I would have if it had been my bridge hand. It healed up okay, but a little crooked, and it never bothered me again except in cold weather.

I want to say that even though the boys in the rackets played rough, everything they did was more or less for a reason. If you horned in on them, or double-crossed them, well, then they would come down on you. There was never any doubt about what would get you into trouble with the mob. But the cops, the cops were a different story entirely. You never knew what those assholes might do. They might arrest you for standing on a corner without a streetcar transfer. Or for playing a game of billiards for a dollar. You had to be awful careful about passing money back and forth in a pool hall. The cops didn't seem to notice that people were getting murdered out on the sidewalk, but try handing a buck to somebody in a pool hall and they would swarm out of the woodwork and slap the cuffs on you. They wanted to look busy for the public. They were trigger-happy, too, which didn't help any.

Here's what I mean. A bunch of us were standing around one night in the United Cigar Store at 63rd and Cottage Grove. It was about 4:30 a.m. We were waiting for the 6:30 edition of the Tribune. There was nothing in it we wanted to read, but it was better than standing around doing nothing. All of a sudden in walked a dopey-looking guy with a broad on his arm. I was drunk, so I said, "What do you suppose she sees in an ugly turd like him?" This was not very smart, as this guy was twice my size and sober.

He whirled around and said, "Who said that?"

Packy MacFarland—good old tough Packy, who knew I wouldn't have a chance—stepped out and said, "I said that."

Right away the guy tore into him, but Packy decked him with one punch. On the floor the guy whipped a gun out of a shoulder holster and shot Packy an inch above the heart. Turned out that the guy was a detective—a plain-clothes copper. Jesus Christ, you think that scene didn't get tense in a hurry . . . but the copper was cool, and he had the drop on all of us. He shot his gun three times in the air for help, he phoned the precinct station, he phoned an ambulance, and he pushed his girl into a cab and got her out of there.

Now all the time Packy was not lying on the floor moaning or anything, he was walking around carrying the bullet that should have been in me, saying things like, "Christ, this hurts. This fucker really hurts."

"Don't worry, Packy, they called an ambulance . . ."

"So what?" he said. "That doesn't mean one is coming."

But one did come, and he was in the hospital for a long time. He finally was okay. There was no trial or anything, even though he had flattened an officer. It cost Packy's old man ten thousand bucks to get the charges dropped. A plain fix. That's the way it was . . . you either had to have money or connections.

Like the time I was driving down Michigan Avenue drunk and knocked a copper off his bicycle. Knocked him clear off the fucking thing. Jesus Christ, he was lying there in the gutter. On 47th Street.

They took me to jail, but all I had to do was say two words and I was out in no time. I don't mean they just waved me out into the street, but I was out of jail before that cop was out of the clinic, I'll say that. The two words were good ones to know, but they wouldn't work for other people, and they didn't always work for me. The words were: "Captain O'Conner." He was my cousin.

In the morning they brought me down to the station house and my cousin gave me a terrible chewing out. In front of a whole bunch of coppers. I would gladly have done thirty days to miss the going over he gave me.

"Drunk!" he said. "You are a disgrace to your family!" he said. "You! You who were supposed to be a priest . . ." he said. I liked that one.

I have done just about everything in the fucking book, but I have never stolen anything or committed murder. Or arson. My main rap has been misdemeanor drunk driving . . . now a felony. But I really should be in the bucket with a lot of other guys.

Not that the cops didn't try to put me there. I was picked up for the Jake Lingel murder. This is no shit. I was coming out of the Tivoli with a girl on my arm when they nabbed me.

"What the fuck is the big idea?" I said to them. "You know I didn't kill anybody."

"We don't know nothing, Danny, except that you are coming along with us."

So I gave my girl a peck and went along with them.

Jake Lingel was a crime reporter for the Tribune. Somebody blew his brains out right on the street in broad daylight, and the town wanted action. The mob has gone too far this time, everybody was saying. Later it came out that Lingel was worth a fortune and must have been on everybody's payroll, but at first the cops had to make a big show of picking up suspects. I had no job, so I was a suspect.

Holy Christ, so was everybody else. That jail was packed. The coppers had gone through the town and swept up everybody on the street that didn't have a transfer.

It was expensive to be in jail. The guards and the turnkeys—"screws," we called them—made a lot of money off of people being held on suspicion. They could lock you up for seventy-two hours with no explanations to anybody. A phone call to your lawyer cost you five bucks. The food they served was absolute shit, but they would get you a hamburger for five bucks. A pot of coffee cost five bucks.

They had so many of us jammed into the jailhouse after the Jake Lingel roust that a lot of guys had to sleep in the hallways outside the cells. Inside it was standing room only. In the cells we took turns sleeping on the floor, half an hour at a time, while the rest of the guys stood and watched. There was room to stretch out in the corridors, so the screws charged a dollar for that.

They even made money on card games, those fucking screws. I watched poker games going on with half of the players inside a cell and half outside. The dealer would go right around the circle, dealing half of the cards between the bars. The stakes weren't big, but the screws took a percentage of the pot just like in a regular gambling joint.

Every so often a dozen guys would be handcuffed or chained and led away for a hearing before a judge. They would tie your ankles together with a chain about two feet long, then run another loop of chain from that up to your handcuffs. I always tried to get them to tie my wrists together at the front instead of behind my back. With your hands in front you could protect yourself a little if some asshole shoved you. A guard might put a hand between your shoulder blades and say, "All right, keep moving," and give you a shove, half of the time right into a wall. I saw many a nose busted that way.

I remember shuffling along trussed up like that while guards jabbed at us with their sticks. "Jesus Christ," I said to one cop, "take it easy. You know we didn't do it."

"Sure, we know you didn't do it, but we have to look good for the public."

"Well, that's fine, but what about us while you are looking good?"

"Oh, don't think about yourselves," this big red-faced prick said, "think about your city."

How do you like that? "Fuck the city," we all said.

"All right, move along," he said, with the big shove.

After the hearing we were all turned loose. Thank God I never had a bum rap pinned on me. Drunk and disorderly, drunk in a public place, drunk driving, and gambling . . . I got nailed on those. Of course, I was always guilty.

After the stock-market crash it really got rough in Chicago. The city was flat broke. Teachers and cops were getting paid with IOU's, that's how bad it got. The worst thing as far as I was concerned was that the cops got a bonus of $200 for killing a bandit, a gangster, a thug, or a holdup man. They got so they would pick up some guy . . . usually a black guy, I am sorry to say . . . put a gun in his hands, and blow his brains out with it. Then they would claim he committed suicide while being arrested. But only cops were eligible for the reward—not honest citizens.

"Shot while trying to escape . . ." was another one they would pull. The idea there was to get the victim to run so they could shoot him in the back. And there was talk that the bonus was going to be raised! If that had gone through there wouldn't have been anybody left in town.

Here is how the "escape" dodge worked. Two cousins of mine, Burt and Jim, who were on the force, gave me the details. They would pick up some poor black bastard and put him in the back of the Cadillac—all the downtown squad cars were Cadillacs.

"What's this all about?" the guy might say. "I didn't do anything."

"Shut up with that shit, you sonofabitch," Burt would say.

"You've been stealing all your life. Well, we finally caught you, and we're going to throw the book at you."

Then Jim would cut in. "Aw, Burt, now listen. He's not such a bad guy. Probably a family man." Giving him the soft con, see? Jim would pretend to be for the guy, pretend to be his friend.

"We're taking him down to the station," Burt would say. "He's no fucking good, ain't never worked a day in his life. He's got nineteen raps against him already."

"No, sir! That's not right! I work all the time . . ."

"Come on, Burt, let's give him a break. He's all right."

"You're always giving these burrheads a break. Why? You got nigger blood in you?"

"Look, Burt, this guy looks okay to me. Let's let him go. Tell you what. We let this one go, and the next one we take down to the station."

"Well, shit," Burt would say, as if he was giving in, "I still think you're too soft on these shines."

That's when Jim would lean back and whisper to the guy, "Listen, when we stop for the light I'm going to unlock your door. I want you to jump out and run like hell down that alley. And don't look back."

Well, they would let the guy get about forty feet away and then they would let him have it. The more witnesses the better. Shot while trying to escape. Did they feel bad about it? Shit, no. They griped about having to split the reward with each other.

I'll never forget "Schemer" Gucci, who was one of Dingbat Oberta's henchmen. I knew him because he used to bet on me once in a while. He got picked up by the Lincoln Squad—the Lincoln Squad drove Lincolns, the Cadillac Squad drove Cadillacs. There were two cops sitting in the front and two in the back. Schemer was between the two cops in back, his right wrist cuffed to one, his left wrist to the other. Those two cops pulled their guns and they both blew his brains out at the same time. Shot attempting to escape, they said. While he was handcuffed to both of them. Do you know that State's Attorney McNaughton cleared those two coppers? Why, they almost got citations for heroism. And when Schemer's old lady came to claim the body there wasn't a penny left in his billfold.

8

Holy
Matrimony

I had three old ladies in the 1920's, two of them by the shotgun route. Right after I got out of the Navy, I took a girl home from a dance and knocked her up. We both felt so bad about it we decided to get married. There was something about me, though, that her father didn't like, so he tried to get it annulled on the grounds of nonperformance of marital duty, which is kind of hard to prove when the bride is pregnant. That led to a trip to The Butcher, after which she was in good shape for the annulment.

Five years later a broad I was running around with missed her monthly flowers and flunked the rabbit test, so it was wedding bells again for me. Her family laid down the law: soon as that kid showed up he would go out for adoption and the young couple would be divorced. I got lucky for once, because after a few months there was a very happy miscarriage. The father hated my guts, but he was a pretty decent guy. He put us in a nice apartment the minute we got married and paid for everything while we waited for the kid. He didn't want his daughter living in a flophouse with me. He paid for the divorce, too. As a matter of fact, when it was all over and I had said good-by to everybody and was on my own again, I figured out that I was about fifteen bucks ahead on the deal.

In about 1927 I married a girl I didn't have to. She was hard to get, which was a challenge, she was nice looking, and she laughed at my jokes. Not only that, she had a job. By 1930, after three years of me, her hair had turned completely gray.

When I first saw her she was at a dance with five other broads. Jesus, it took me all night to bust those six apart and get at the one I wanted. And when I finally got her she held me off for months before I finally scored. I admired her for that—it made me feel pretty sure that not too many other people had been on base. I started thinking of marrying her pretty early, because I was spending too goddam much time chasing pussy. With a broad of my own at home I could concentrate on my billiards. But I made sure I scored before getting married—I didn't want to wind up with a broad who didn't get her ass off the sheets.

We were lying in bed one day and I said, "What do you say we get married?" I had been looking at the ceiling, comparing her salary with my expenses, and I decided we could squeak by.

"Sounds like a good idea to me," she said.

As soon as we had the marriage license we climbed on a double-decker bus and rode downtown to the courthouse, where about fifty white, black, and Chinese guys tried to hustle us into this judge or that one. It was quite a carnival the way those judges fought for business.

After the ceremony, which took at least a minute, we strolled into Henrici's, which is a very nice restaurant on Randolph Street between Dearborn and Clark. It was strictly high class. Even in those days a baked potato cost fifty cents, and you didn't get any aluminum foil. We ordered steaks, but we hardly touched them.

We were holding hands and billing and cooing like a couple of high school kids. I don't know what it is about getting married, but for a while there you feel happy. I made up my mind to settle down and get a job and be a good husband to this broad, who was a very square apple but a hell of a nice person.

The next day I got a job and we moved into an apartment in the Tudor Arms for $120 a month, which is like $500 today. We were right close to the Illinois Central electric train, which got you downtown in twenty minutes flat. You were flying on that sonofabitch, doing eighty or ninety miles an hour. You couldn't even finish Moon Mullins before the conductor was shouting: "Randolph Street . . ."

Everything was wonderful, but I started chasing pussy on the side. Don't ask me why. I had the lay of the land at home, but there I was galavanting around town with my old cronies. I was the biggest chippy in town, and I'm not proud of it.

One night I said to my old lady, "I'm going out with Gordon Thexton tonight, dear. We are going to make some of the billiard rooms and see what is going on."

"All right, dear," she said. She was never suspicious and never hounded me. It got to be quite aggravating. "I think I will go over to mother's."

"Good idea," I said. "See you later."

Now this Gordon Thexton is the same one who got my nose broken when I spun that steak across the floor. He was about five foot three and his folks were rich. He loved a good time and he thought I was the greatest. All I had to do was sneeze and he went into hysterics.

Gordon was waiting for me on a side street in his Cadillac and his raccoon coat, a broad at his side. In the back seat was another raccoon coat and broad for me. My God, with that crazy Gordon we were in trouble inside an hour.

After loading up on bathtub gin at the Coconut Grove, we went to Chan's Silver Slipper, a big Chinese restaurant with a dance floor and band. The Silver Slipper was a fancy joint—I mean the band had both a male and a female singer who had nothing to do but sing. No doubling on the tuba or any of that shit.

All the help wore tuxedos, and for some reason Gordon thought it would be funny to sprinkle soy sauce on our waiter's boiled shirt. He shook the little glass bottle and that beetle-juice came out real good for him, all over the waiter's starched vest. Well, holy shit, I was well known in the joint, even well liked, but next thing I know we are paying for a meal we didn't finish eating and we are being thrown down the stairs. I was higher than a kite, and as I landed on the sidewalk I thought it was quite a big joke.

When we were all together, we headed for Gordy's car, and as we passed the O'Conner and Goldberg shoe store, which was right under the night club, who do you suppose was standing there looking into the window? My wife and my mother-in-law!

"Don't anybody say 'Danny,' " I hissed at Gordon and the girls. "Don't anybody say anything!"

So Gordy said, "Hey, Danny, where is the nearest bootlegging joint?"

The two women rounded and looked me right in the eye. My mother-in-law gave out with a gasp that would be worth a million on tape today. I am hard to embarrass, but that turned me red.

We kept on going. Gordy, he didn't give a shit, and the two broads we were with gave a shit less. We went over to some goddam speakeasy and sat there drinking gin. I had a face three feet long. The more I drank the lousier I felt. And my date was a pushover, that was another thing. "Anytime you're ready," was her policy. I could have had her in the car, while we were sitting in the back seat. I could have swung her over me and sat her on the peg, but I had lost all interest in that. All I could think of was the looks on the faces of my old lady and her mother.

At about two in the morning we dropped my broad off at her

place. I hadn't touched her. Then I had to sit in the car and wait while Gordy gave his broad a wiggle in the front seat. Finally he took me home.

"We had a hell of a night tonight, eh, Dan?" he said.

"Yeah, we sure did."

I went inside and tried the door of the apartment. The chain wasn't hooked. I pushed the door open . . .

My wife had the habit of sitting on the overstuffed chair reading a Diamond Dick novel with her feet tucked under her. That's the way I found her. At about three fucking o'clock in the morning. What she said to me really put me down. Put me down so bad I didn't even speak to another broad for a whole year.

"Did you have a nice time, Dan?"

That's all. She put a little leaflet in her book and closed it. Didn't slam it shut, just closed it. "Did you have a nice time, Dan?" is what she said, in a quiet voice. Jesus Christ, if she had called me a sonofabitch, a dirty rotten bastard, chewed my ass out, I would have felt twice as good about it. But that "Did you have a nice time, Dan?" really killed me.

She never got mad, which irked the hell out of me. Well, she did get mad once. She sent me down to the corner store for a loaf of rye bread, and a week later I phoned her from Cincinnati and said: "They don't have rye." Yes, that pissed her off.

I did even worse than that to her . . . to a girl who always was good to me. I breezed into the apartment one night with two broads, threw one on the couch and one into the bed with her, then climbed into bed between them. It was nothing I planned or meant to do—there was just no other way. I was out with Gordon again, and as a joke he disappeared and left us with a big cab bill. He knew I didn't have a nickel, or the broads either. The only thing I could figure out to do was to ask the cabby to stop in front of a hotel a block away from my apartment.

"Pull over here for a minute, driver, the girls have to go in and take a pee. I'll wait with you here in the cab."

He pulled over and the girls got out. So did I, and I hustled those two broads into an empty lot next to the hotel and we made a run for it. The cabby jumped out and started chasing us, so we had to turn on the speed. He gave up after a few minutes, because it was pitch dark and he didn't know his way around the neighborhood. The girls lost their shoes going across the field, but I couldn't help that.

I had to get those girls out of sight. I couldn't leave them screaming on a street corner. Running out on a cab bill was a serious offense, the same as defrauding an innkeeper, and was worth six months in the county jail. All I could do was take them to my apartment.

It was about three in the morning again. My old lady was in bed pretending to be asleep, but I could see how tight her mouth was when I threw that one broad in the sack and climbed in after her.

Here is the capper: In the morning the alarm went off and who was the only one who got up? My wife. She made breakfast for all of us. Nobody said much. The two broads weren't embarrassed at all, and they ate a big breakfast. Oh, yes, those skunks ate, all right.

When they were gone, wearing some of my old lady's shoes, I told her more or less the truth. "We just meant to go on a little ride through Washington Park, and one thing led to another."

"Oh," she said. She was completely calm. She had her arms crossed looking at me, and I had a head that was ringing like a gong. "Danny," she said, "why do you do these things?"

I was very arrogant in those days. People who think I am arrogant now haven't seen anything. I thought I was Mr. Shit and that everything I did had to be right. But that particular day I knew I was in the wrong. I wanted to level with my old lady when she asked me why I did those things, but I didn't know myself.

"I don't know," I said. "You got me there."

But she wasn't mad, that was the terrible part. Talk about aggravating! That's when I decided I had to get out of Chicago. My old lady was beginning to drive me nuts. I told her that I would hustle my way out to the coast and when I lit someplace I would send for her.

She loved me, I guess, the poor bastard, probably still does. That was her problem. I had caused her nothing but trouble, but when I left she was crying tears as big as horse turds.

Part Two

•

ON THE MOVE

•

1929–1954

9

Seeing
America
by
Train

I had to get out of Chicago, and not just because of my wife. I wasn't getting anywhere, wasn't making anything of myself. The Depression had started, and it was almost impossible to get a job, which I had to do every once in a while to pay my bills. The boys I knew in the rackets were after me to make some easy money, and the cops were always hanging around trying to pin things on me.

It began to sink in that Chicago was no place for me when I was caught in the net that the cops threw out after the St. Valentine's Day Massacre. They held me in jail for a couple of days along with a thousand other guys and I didn't enjoy it at all. I knew it was just for show, but you never could be sure how far they would go. Lots of guys are in the bucket right today for things they didn't do. When the cops started getting bonuses for plugging people—well, that did it. I was leaving.

My mother. I hadn't seen my mother in over ten years. My

plan was to hop freights going west, hustle pool in all the little towns, and pay a surprise visit to my mother. I had a rich uncle in San Francisco, too, who had some kind of mining deal going in Tonopah, Nevada. Things would perk up when I saw my mother and uncle, I figured. Jobs were scarce, but they would be glad to see me and they would be able to figure out something for me to do. There is nothing like blood relatives when the chips are down.

Another guy who wanted to get moving was Ray Mauer, a card player and dice man. We decided to travel together, at least for a while, stopping first at the Illinois State Fair in Springfield. There were jobs to be had there, we were told, all kinds of carnival-type jobs, and there would be millions of marks walking around with their mouths open and twenty-dollar bills sticking out of all their pockets. A few weeks in Springfield and we would both have nice bankrolls for the long trip west.

It was 1:08 in the morning when Ray Mauer and I got on the Seminole Limited, a very high-class passenger train, at 63rd and Dorchester, the first stop out of the Loop. I remember the time because 108 was my badge number when I was driving cab. I had on a brown silk shirt, cream-colored pants, an expensive pair of brown and white oxfords, and a straw hat that I lost about a hundred yards down the track. That's how I was dressed when I got on the Seminole Limited, which is one of the stupider things I have done in my life. What was stupid about getting on a passenger train dressed like that? Nothing, except that we got on the coal car. The coal car! It was the only car that had anything we could catch onto. Up the ladder we went, jumping down on the coal pile at the back end, as far away from the cab of the engine as we could get. We thought we could just stand there for the short run down to Springfield without getting too dirty. Of course, we were drunk, which didn't help any. All we had between us was two flat fifths of Panther Piss.

As the train started pulling out, it got obvious that we were going to be spotted any minute by the fireman and engineer. We were in plain view, even when we crouched down. Getting thrown off the train wouldn't have been so bad—what we were worried about was that we would be made to shovel coal into the firebox all the way to Springfield while the fireman sat on his ass and played his harmonica.

"Dig in," Ray said, "we've got to dig in."

So we got down and pulled coal over ourselves until only our heads showed. We kept one arm out, too, so we could pass the alky back and forth. It was the shits, but it was the only thing we could see to do. When we got to Springfield we would have to wash up and get our clothes cleaned, but that was a cheap enough price to pay for a free ride on the Seminole Limited.

Now before we got on we made sure that that baby went to Springfield. "Does this train go to Springfield?" we asked half a dozen people who were hanging around the platform.

"Yes, sir," they all said, "this train goes right through Spring-field."

It went through Springfield, all right, but at about ninety miles an hour.

"Shouldn't we be there by now?" I asked Ray after we had been buried in the coal pile for a couple of hours.

"We are due in any minute."

"Well, I hate to tell you, but this bastard isn't slowing down. This bastard is going faster all the time. Those lights we passed a while back. That was Springfield."

"Oh, Jesus, no!"

It was six hours before the train stopped, and when it did it was in East St. Louis. We almost froze to death along the way. When we climbed down from that coal car we looked like the wreck of the Hesperus—a couple of drunken chimney sweeps.

But hard knocks and bum steers like that seemed to be the only way to learn how to ride trains. The old-timers gave out all sorts of goofy advice. Not on purpose, I don't think, but because they didn't want to admit they didn't know the right answers. If you are a hobo and you don't know how to get where you are going by train, you aren't worth much, are you? So they would pretend they knew and tell you what to do, and half the time they were wrong.

"You want the train to Nashville, son? Then stand by that water tank. The train that stops there is the train to Nashville."

Shit, you get on that train and you might end up in Waukegan. It was awful hard to get the right information. You couldn't ask anybody who worked for the railroad, naturally, or you would be put in the bucket. There weren't any signs saying: "Southbound bums board here." You had to watch out for the railroad dicks, too, who were mean as hell and armed with clubs. They loved nothing better than to cover your head with big knobs. I went through the tortures of hell traveling with Ray Mauer, who knew less than I did, which was nothing.

When we got off the train in East St. Louis I looked like Al Jolson made up for one of his famous scenes. Hitching a ride on a passenger train, oh, that made the railroads boil. They considered that the height of guts. Soon as we hit the ground and started stumbling toward the station, a big road dick grabbed me by the collar and said, "Just where in the fuck do you think *you're* going?"

"I'm getting the hell out of *here*, I can tell you that," I said. I didn't know exactly who the guy was, but I knew he was cop. He was cop all over.

"You sure as hell are," he said. "You are coming with me. And you are coming, too," he said to Ray. Now Ray was not a meek man, but he kept his mouth shut. That dick had me by the seat of the pants and the back of the neck and he marched me on my tiptoes to the depot. "You no-good Irish prick," he said, "you are going to buy a ticket and get on the next train back to Chicago."

We didn't have the money, so he took us to the Western Union office and made me wire my aunts for some. I had to put up my wrist watch before they would send a collect telegram. We had to sit outside on the curb waiting for an answer—they wouldn't even let us inside the goddam place, we looked so awful. After a while the money came in. Ten bucks, I think it was. When I had it in my hand, I walked over to the bull and said, "Look, I know you think we are a couple of bums or something like that . . ."

"I sure as hell do think you are a couple of bums or something like that."

"Listen, give us a break. We like to froze to death on that coal car. We didn't know we were coming here—we meant to get off at Springfield. Somebody told us the train went through Springfield, and, brother, he wasn't lying. It went right through Springfield. We were drunk. Look, there is a flophouse across the street. Let us clean up over there and sleep it off. We'll be on the first train in the morning back to Chicago."

There is something about my face. I have always looked younger than I am. "All right," he said, "but don't try to double-cross me."

"Don't worry."

We got a room for fifty cents and slept for pretty near a day. When we woke up I said to Ray, "How do you feel?"

"Lousy," he said.

"Tell you what. Heads we go back to Chicago, tails we keep going west."

"Suits me."

It was tails. We headed west.

We had to go *eighteen miles* west before we could get on another train. We couldn't hang around and do any hustling or gambling, either, because if that railroad bull spotted us it would have been our asses. We sneaked around the depot, keeping our eyes peeled. An old-timer we ran into gave us a good steer. He told us that eighteen miles to the west was hump that made the trains slow way down. We could *walk* and get on. He was right. After riding streetcars and city buses and walking for a few miles we found the long grade. First train by we climbed on a nice empty gondola car—not a hopper car, which has a sloping bottom. In a hopper car you practically have to hang by your fingernails to keep from sliding down and out through the trapdoor gates in the bottom. No, we were in a clean, flat-bottomed gondola. We sat in the front corners with our backs to the engine. That way the wind is not in your face and you don't get so much soot in your eyes.

We thought we had it made then, thought our troubles were over, but when it got dark we were in hot water again. The train started to slow down. I pulled myself up to the top edge of the side and took a look around. We were in the middle of nowhere—no town, no water tank, nothing. From the next car we could hear some other hobo say, "God, I wonder how many guys they want this time." It was a roust. A posse had stopped the train—a couple of dozen cops, prison guards, sheriff's deputies, and whatnot, some on horses and some in trucks. I found out later that every once in a while posses would stop the freights and make every poor sonofabitch get off. It might be the railroad's doing, just to make life miserable for the hobos, or it might be the cops looking for some particular thief or runaway con, or it might just be a local rancher or politician who wanted a gang to work on a road and knew how to get one free.

It was not only dark, there were patches of fog close to the ground, and you could see clouds of it blowing through the headlight beams from the trucks. We were outside a penitentiary somewhere in Missouri. There were about a hundred people riding the train, and we all had to line up so they could look us over. Guys on horseback carrying rifles came along and shined flashlights in our faces, and other guys on foot went through our pockets. They picked out three colored guys and two whites and put them in a truck. The rest of us started making moves to get back on the train, but the big boss—I suppose he was the sheriff—put an end to that. "Say good-by to the train, you assholes," he hollered, "and start marching across that field."

According to him there was a highway about a mile away. We moved out, through bushes and weeds. We were right next to the pen, and we could look up at the high walls and see the searchlights and turrets and guards looking down at us. "All right, all right, shake it up, come on," the sheriff shouted. We weren't going fast enough to suit him. I suppose he had a wife at home trying to keep a big dinner warm. The whole bunch of us stumbled across the field, including five or six women. When we got to the road we all looked at each other like we just got the death sentence. Highway, the guy had said, but it was just two dirt ruts across a godforsaken piece of nowhere.

Then we heard the engine give off two hoots, which meant the train was about to start rolling again. We could see the headlights of the trucks and hear the horses moving down the line away from us. We all got the same idea at once: get back on the train. Everybody headed back across the field without a word, hoping to get to the train before it picked up too much speed. It takes a long time for a hundred-car train to get going, so quite a few of us made it. None of the old people did, though, and only one or two of the women, but everybody tried their damnedest, crashing through the weeds, falling down and getting up—to be stuck out there in the middle of Missouri would have been murder. It probably would have meant a twenty- or thirty-mile hike down the tracks to the next water tank, or to some other spot where the trains stopped or slowed down.

I was fast on my feet, thank God. A lot of times I got out of trouble in pool halls after hustling somebody out of his lunch money by just running out the front door and outdistancing the pack. Fleet-footed Dan, they called me for a while. But fast as I was, the train was going at least fifteen miles an hour when I got to it, which is a hell of a speed. I have heard people say they have hopped freights going thirty miles an hour, but such people are full of shit. I ran as fast as I could alongside the cars, trying to catch up to one, but I was already pooped from going across the field. The cars were shooting past me and getting faster all the time, so I knew I had to make a stab at it now or never. You don't try for a ladder at the back of a car, because if you miss you fall between the cars. I dove for a ladder at the front, caught hold, and was given a terrific wrench, but I hung on. My legs kept getting swept out from under me and I almost didn't have enough strength to get my foot up to the bottom rung, but I finally made it.

I climbed the ladder. It was a sealed boxcar, so I had to ride on top, which meant I had the wind on me all night and couldn't sleep or even relax. I had no idea if Ray had made it or not, but I wasn't about to go looking for him. I didn't have the nerve to go hopping from one car to another the way some 'bo's did.

When it got light I could see from one end of the train to another, and I counted about twenty-five people. I saw Ray about five cars behind me. We waved to each other and got off at the first town.

Whenever I tell people about riding freights they always seem amazed that as many as a hundred people might be on a train at once. Hell, that was nothing. I've been on freights that were carrying two hundred hobos, two hundred and fifty, even. All kinds of people. In the Depression an awful lot of people were broke and were going someplace else hoping to find better luck, or to run out on debts, or to go live with relatives. Without money, riding the rails was the only way to go, especially in the West. Hitchhiking was too slow. There weren't enough good roads or fast traffic.

It got to be a way of life for some guys—always on the move. Always looking for something—they couldn't have told you what. They didn't even know where they were going exactly, most of the time. Ask them and they would say, "West," or, "East." That's all. Not the name of any place.

There were migratory workers, following the harvest. Heading for Washington in the fall to pick apples, stuff like that. But then there were guys who would be going in the opposite direction, trying to get as far away as possible from where the work was being done. Time to pick lettuce in California? Then they would be in North Carolina. I was pretty much like that myself. Work was strictly a last resort. Things had to be awful tough.

Things did get awful tough—too tough for Ray. We did just well enough hustling to stay alive, but not much more. We used the lemonade, the dump, the double dump, every trick in the book, but the pickings were slim. I would usually go in the room first and play by myself. He would come in an hour later and "win" a few bucks from me, then quit. If none of the local marks took the bait he would urge them: "Go on, you can beat that ass-hole. He dropped a fin to me and I can't play a lick." The old line.

One reason the hustling was hard was because we had so little money. I had no chance to gamble away a few bucks to set a guy up for a kill. Lots of time I had to play on my nerve, without a penny in my pocket. We would wake up in the morning in some flophouse kicking the wolf in the mouth, flat broke. Not even enough for a cup of coffee and a sinker. The minute the local pool hall was open we would be there and I would be hitting somebody up for a game of pool. Hungry, so hungry sometimes I could hardly stand it.

"Sure, I'll play you a game, mister," a guy says to me one morning, "but not for money. Let's just play for fun."

Jesus Christ, my stomach is screaming for food, and he wants to play hee-haw! But that's the sort of thing you run into in those one-turd towns.

Ray got no action at all. Never once did we find a card game or a dice game. He tried to start some craps going, but had no luck. This was too bad, because he had a way of holding one dice on the outside of the cup with his little finger and letting it go with the others so it wouldn't turn over, which made him a mortal lock to win. But nobody would roll with him. He gave up, finally, and went back to Chicago. I liked Ray, but I was glad to see him go. Two strangers were too obvious in a small town. Alone, I figured, I couldn't possibly do any worse, and, by God, after he left I started making some scores. The best one was in El Dorado, Kansas.

I had smartened up considerably, knew how to travel. It was about ten at night when I wheeled off a "mop." "Mop" is what we called the Missouri-Pacific Railroad. I wheeled off a side-door Pullman and hiked down to the depot. They didn't stop freights in front of the depot to make it easy for the bums, you know. Christ, sometimes we were miles from the depot. I was wearing coveralls, with the sleeves and pants cuffs tied with cord to keep the dirt out, and the neck tied tight with a bandanna. In the depot can I peeled off the coveralls. Underneath I was wearing a complete suit of clothes—white shirt, tie, handkerchief in the chest pocket, the whole works. All I had to do was wash my face and hands and wipe off my shoes and I was ready for anything. The whole process took me only about ten minutes, including stashing my coveralls, razor, and toothbrush in the bushes.

I walked up the main drag. About three thousand population, I figured . . . not big enough to have a player who could give me any trouble. Into the pool hall I went. Every town had one. Now I was hungry, understand what I mean? Hadn't eaten for pretty near a day. Didn't have a penny on me.

The room was like a lot of others, a long line of beat-up pool tables with low lights over them, each one with a green metal shade. Spittoons in the corners covered with crust. To the guy behind the counter I said, "You got anybody here who wants a game of pool?" I had no time to fuck around. I needed a score fast.

"Some of the boys in the back might want to play a little pastime," the guy said.

"Listen," I said, "I don't play hee-haw. I'm looking for somebody who wants to make it interesting."

"Ohhhhhhhhh. You're a good player, is that it?"

"I sure as hell am." The direct approach. Somebody would be curious enough to play me a game just to see if I was kidding.

"Get Lem," the bartender said, nodding to a bunch of guys

who were standing there eyeing me. Lem was the local shark, a barber by trade, best player in seven counties, and people flew out the door looking for him. Everybody wanted to see some action. This was El Dorado, Kansas, remember, where not a hell of a lot happens.

Fifteen minutes later in walked a guy, tall and thin. He looked like he could be a player.

"I hear you want to play a little pool," he said.

"That's right," I said, "but not for less than three dollars."

Three dollars was quite a bit in the Depression. For three dollars you could get ham hocks and beans, a fifth of giggle soup, a hotel room with a window, and maybe a hoor or two besides.

"Get your cue," he said.

He didn't seem afraid at all. He picked out his favorite table, one where he knew all the hills and dales, while I tried to find a decent cue in the rack. It took me quite a while to find one that wasn't left behind by W. C. Fields. Fifty points of line-up straight pool, we decided. For three dollars, and me without a red cent. To show you how cocky I was in those days, I bummed a cigarette off the guy.

I won the lag and made him break. As I was chalking my cue, who walked in the door but the town clown. The constable. The door-shaker. He was probably the only cop the town had, but he was big . . . about six-foot-six . . . and he stood three feet from the end of the table, looking me over. He wasn't wearing a uniform, just a police cap and work clothes, and a long billy-club that he held in his hand. He rocked back and forth, back and forth. I missed my first shot so far I banked it in the side.

Everything started running through my mind. I would be tarred and feathered and run out of town on a rail. Or they would put me on the chain gang to do road work for a few years. First thing I knew I was behind forty-three to eight, my shot with nothing open. It was hopeless, so I decided to take a powder, get the hell out of there. I would head for the hobo jungle down by the tracks and hope that they would give me a bite to eat. I hated to go into a jungle empty-handed, though. You were supposed to contribute something to the stew.

I laid my cue on the table. "I have to take a leak," I said. "Where's the pisser?"

It was in the back end of the room. I didn't have to take a leak, but I walked up to the urinal and stood there. My idea was to go out the back window, but it was barred. Bars the size of your finger. There was no way, I mean there was no way to get out. The back door, I thought. I would come out of the pisser and shoot through the back door. With a head start of fifty feet, Fleet-footed Dan could lose himself in the night. But the back door had a huge plank nailed across it. Nailed solid. With the right tools I could have pried it off in about a week.

On my way back to the table I thought, "Well, you dumb bastard, you got yourself into it this time. Your luck has run out." I had played on my nerve many times before and always was fortunate.

I shot a deliberate safety. That put him off a little, because he fouled when trying to return it. Then I took a deliberate foul, just touching the tip of my cue to the ball. He scratched again, trying not to break up the balls. I took another deliberate, leaving him corner-hooked. Trying to play safe—which was not his game at all—he scratched again, and that cost him fifteen points. There was a little argument about that, but it is right in the rule book: three scratches in a row costs you fifteen points. That dropped the score to 25–6; I was back in the ball game.

I got another lucky break then—the town clown left. He wasn't interested in games where the players jacked off playing safe. That made me feel better, and I started to make balls. All the other action in the joint stopped; everybody was watching our game. I really didn't know if I would be better off losing or winning. That crowd didn't look very friendly.

The final score was 50–40—I beat him after needing 42 when

he only needed 7. But the amazing thing was this: when I made the last ball the place went wild—cheering and yelling, everybody shaking my hand, slapping me on the back, telling me how great I played. It was fantastic. Turns out that everybody hated Lem the Barber. Lem had been taking their money for years. They had been waiting for somebody, hoping for somebody to come to town who could beat him.

One young kid came over to me and grabbed me and shook my hand and said, "Jeez, that was great. Where you headed?"

"West."

"Are you in the local hotel?"

"Well, no, I haven't had a chance to check in yet."

"Come on out to the house, then. How would you like a home-cooked meal and a warm bed? When pa hears what you did tonight he'll kill me if I don't bring you home." Oh, how they hated the barber in that town.

I went with that kid and met his family. They honestly seemed to like me. Of course, they hated the barber. I stayed with them for five days, eating all I could and sleeping late. Then one day the father came home with a big smile and said to me: "Wonderful news, Dan! I've got a job for you with Standard Oil. You start tomorrow."

"Gee, thanks," I said. "That certainly is wonderful news."

Before dawn the next morning I was tiptoeing out of the house on my way to the railroad yard. An hour later I was on a rattler headed for El Paso.

10

Seeing More America by Train

It was night. I was half asleep, but I knew the train was coming to a stop because of the way it was rattling and squealing and groaning. I didn't really wake up until the flashlight was in my face. Another roust.

"Where you from?" the guy behind the light said.

"Chicago," I said, hoping I didn't look like the local escaped rapist.

"Okay," he said, "sorry to bother you."

"Where are we?"

"Next stop is Amarillo."

He jumped out of my boxcar and climbed in the next one. Half an hour later we were rolling again. Things like that happened quite often—cops stopping trains looking for somebody. I was passed by in this case because the cop knew I was telling the truth when I said I was from Chicago. The guy he wanted was from someplace else. He could tell from the way I said

"Chicago," from my accent, that I wasn't lying. Some of those railroad bulls, especially the border guards, were amazing, they were so good at pinpointing accents. I guess it makes sense that they were good at it, because they spent all their time rousting bums from everywhere, but it was still amazing. Why, a guy could shout, "Shit!" and have those bulls holler, "Philadelphia!"

I made the hobo jungle in Amarillo, but it wasn't much. I didn't care for it. Too many Mexicans. Not that they bothered me, exactly; it was just that they stuck together and didn't make me feel like they were glad I was there. But I did learn how to say, "Mucho trabajo, poco dinero." I spent my last couple of bucks on a fifth of booze and some meat for the jungle stew. I slept all right. When you make it plain that you are busted you don't have to worry about getting robbed. In the morning I was on the first train out.

Between Amarillo and El Paso the route passes through Carrizozo, New Mexico, and by the time we stopped there I was starving. I was so hungry I knew I wouldn't be able to stand spending hours trying to hustle somebody in a pool hall. At the last couple of water stops the towns didn't even have pool halls, they were so little and poor, yet the other hobos climbed back on the train with all kinds of stuff to eat. I knew how they did it—they begged at back doors. I never thought I would stoop that low, never thought I would be that hungry. But I had to do something. I made up my mind to be first off the train at the next stop. I was bound and determined to get something to eat no matter what I had to do.

As we slowed down for Carrizozo, I swung off my flatcar and trotted across a field toward a white house at the edge of town. When I banged on that back door with the flat of my hand— bang, bang, bang—I knew I had hit bottom. I was a bum and couldn't deny it. Nobody answered at first, but I could hear a washing-machine motor going somewhere inside, so I knew somebody was at home. Bang, bang, bang! A gray-haired lady stuck her head out of a window.

"What's on your mind, son?" she said.

"Look, lady, I hate to bother you, honest I do, but I am so hungry I can't stand it. Is there any work I could do for you to earn a little something to eat? I am really hungry. God, I am really hungry."

"You look hungry . . ."

"There is no kidding about it. I'll do anything."

"Well," she said, after looking at me for awhile, "there is nothing that needs doing around here right now. I've already picked the apples. But I'll tell you what . . . wait till I dry my hands . . ."

A few minutes later she opened the back door and gave me a note to the grocer down the street: "Give this young man whatever he wants and charge it to me."

I thanked her about fifty times and then made a beeline for the store. I went wild—I took a carton of cigarettes, a ring of sausage, a loaf of bread, a bunch of bananas. I made it back to the train just as it was pulling out, carrying a sack of groceries higher than my head.

You might think I knocked on doors from then on, but I didn't. It made me feel too low. It made me feel like I had no pride left at all. In the next couple of years, even though I was awful hard up at times, I only begged for food once or twice. I would rather slave over a hot pool table for twenty-four hours than spend five minutes begging for food.

About twenty miles out of El Paso a hobo gave me a piece of advice. "Don't go into El Paso," he said. "Get off at the junction outside of town, or even before. El Paso is the worst. They catch you there and you will be elected to help move a mountain of rock with a nice chain around your ankle."

But I was too groggy to pay much attention to him. Ten minutes asleep, twenty minutes awake, five minutes asleep . . . It's awful hard to sleep while you are getting bounced around on a flatcar, wind and soot in your face, afraid you might roll over the side if you forget where you are. I must have dozed off for quite a while, because all of a sudden I realized that the train was giving that lurch and shudder that it does when it comes to a stop. I felt the engine break off from the cars. Now I can't explain how I knew that the engine was breaking off, but you can tell when it happens; everything goes completely dead. Then it hit me! I jumped to my feet. We were parked in downtown El Paso! Right in the plaza! In the middle of a street! Holy Christ, I had to get out of there . . .

There were buildings and streetlights all around, but it was pretty dark near my car. I eased myself over the side, real slow, real slow, put my feet on the gravel alongside the tracks without making a sound, then started moving away from that goddam train . . .

"Hold it!"

I froze and heard footsteps come up behind me. A hand twisted the back of my collar and another hand frisked me, patting me all over. "Who are you?" the guy said, turning me around and putting a flashlight on me.

"Nobody, sir," I said, very polite. I managed to unbutton the collar of my coveralls so he could see my shirt and tie.

"Where you headed?"

"I'm trying to get to San Francisco, sir."

He shook his head back and forth. "Well, you've got more goddam nerve than any punk I've ever seen. Didn't anybody tell you not to ride into this town?"

"No, sir. Nobody told me. I didn't mean to stop here. I don't even know what this town is, sir." I was trying to give the best impression I could, that I was a decent young kid and not your average bum. I was thirty years old at the time, but I only looked about twenty, which helped. I was plenty scared, because this bull could have done anything he wanted to me, could have put me right on the road gang.

"Well, I'll be goddammed," he said. "Got any money?"

"No, sir."

"Hungry?"

He was melting. "Oh, God, mister, I'm awful hungry." A couple of hours before I had eaten an entire bunch of bananas and was so full I was ready to puke.

"Okay. See that building on the corner? See the door with the light over it? Go in there and they'll fix you up."

I thanked him and went down to the building on the corner, which was a big warehouse sort of a place. Inside the door was a desk, and I was staring at a fucking Sergeant of Police. "Name? Place of birth? Occupation? Destination? Any itching diseases?" He wrote it all down, then told me to take a shower and have something to eat.

I took off my clothes. Along one wall was a row of high faucets, just faucets without shower heads. The water was cold, but not ice cold. The Sergeant watched every move I made. He didn't want me stealing the soap by sticking it in my rosette. "Wash out your shorts and socks," he said, so I did, hanging them on a hook and putting my shoes and pants on without them. Now I could have some stew. It was mostly beans but there was quite a bit of pork floating around in there, and it wasn't half bad. My appetite came back, and I ate a whole bowl. I saw another derelict go for seconds, so I did, too.

Into an Army cot I went. It was about four in the morning. There were a dozen guys in cots, snoring away. One blanket and no pillow, but I wasn't complaining.

In the morning they spilled us onto the floor at seven o'clock sharp. After another bowl of stew they lined us up on the sidewalk in the blinding sunshine—and a grubby bunch we were— and a brand new Sergeant read a fucking proclamation to us. This is the honest-to-God truth. "The City of El Paso in the great State of Texas has been kind enough to see you through your hour of adversity and wishes you well as you continue on your journey . . ." In other words, get moving, you assholes.

I got moving across the border to Juarez, which I had heard a lot about. I drifted into a joint called The Great American Bar. I think it's still there. Lined up at the rail was a row of Texas ranchers, big guys with ten-gallon hats. This was in the Depression, but every one of them had a pile of money in front of him.

God, I had guts in those days. I walked right in and elbowed my way to the bar.

"What are you drinking?" the bartender said, wondering if he should pitch me out on my ass.

I said, "Gee, I'd sure like a nice glass of cold water."

The rancher on my right was giving me the once-over. He said, "Hey, kid, don't you know water rusts out the stomach?" It was 1931 and that joke was old then, but I gave him a big hee-haw just the same. He asked me where I was from, and when I said Chicago he had some fun with me. "Where's your Tommy gun? How many gangsters have you killed?" All that shit.

I told them I was on my way to see my mother in San Francisco and was riding freights because I didn't have any money. I never could have made them believe that story if it hadn't been true.

"Riding freights?" one guy said. "Why, that's dangerous."

"That's no way for a young fellow like you to travel," another one said. "You might fall in with a low class of people."

All my life I've had a miserable frown on my face—unless I was getting drunk. A first-class sourpuss. The Sunshine Kid, Shamrock Eakin used to call me. But I had an honest Irish mug that has been a help to me. In fact, somebody told me years ago that I had a pleasing personality. I don't know what ever happened to it.

When I walked out of that bar in Juarez I had fifty dollars cash in my pocket. Those ranchers had taken up a collection so I could go see my mother on a passenger train. One of them had even phoned across the river to El Paso to find out what the fare was to San Francisco. But did I have sense enough to buy a ticket?

Hell, no. Four hours later I was the drunkest skunk west of the Pecos. I met a drinking buddy. When you want somebody to drink with and you have some money, you always find him. Sure enough, I met some thirsty donkey on a street corner and away we went.

When I finally dragged myself aboard a westbound boxcar I was not only broke, I had a pounding hangover besides.

The hobo jungle at Colton, California, was one of the biggest in the country. Maybe the biggest. Colton was a junction point for three railroads, the Santa Fe, the Union Pacific, and the Southern Pacific. I might have missed it, but all the 'bo's on my train told me I would be crazy if I did, that it was a fantastic place. They weren't kidding. Even today I enjoy meeting an old-timer that remembers the Colton jungle.

I got there at night. As the train eased along, slowing down, I didn't see three bonfires, I didn't see ten bonfires, or fifteen; I saw thirty, at least. I hopped off even though I didn't have a lump, a taw, something to contribute. I walked all around with my eyes wide open. I was hungry and I could smell coffee and stew and burning wood. There were half a dozen guys sitting or crouching around each fire, cooking or just talking. There was laundry strung out on ropes.

A river ran through the place, and there were signs telling you where to wash dishes, where to take a bath, where to wash clothes. There were rules, and, by God, you better abide by them.

Ironing boards were built right into trees, with old-fashioned flatirons that you had to heat in the fire. Tree trunks were covered with hundreds of shiny pie tins hanging on nails. Pie tins were what everybody ate out of, and they were kept spotlessly clean. Nobody owned them—they just stayed in the camp. Pie tins, tin cups, and spoons—that's all you used to eat with, just like in the Big Joint . . . the penitentiary.

I saw no shanties or lean-tos, and later I found out why. The sheriff wouldn't allow them—he wouldn't allow anybody to stay more than two days. Every morning he walked through the jungle looking each man in the face. If he recognized you from the day before he would say, "My friend, you are ready to move on. Good luck to you." The town knew that they couldn't stop the bums from coming in, so they tried only to control the situation. It was smart of them, and the sheriff wasn't a bad guy.

As I walked around the first night I saw piles and piles of watermelon, potatoes, tomatoes, onions, all kinds of fruit and vegetables. One of the things you had to do to stay there was make a contribution, so there were guys fanning out at all times stealing stuff from the surrounding farms and orchards, or asking the local bakers, butchers, and citizens for handouts. Meat was the big problem; you had to rely on the butchers for scraps, but they usually came through. "Nickel up on the butcher," was the way they described it, I guess because you would tell him that you didn't have a nickel but were hungry just the same.

I stood in the shadows about six feet from one of the biggest bonfires, where they had a five-gallon can of stew cooking. One guy was in charge of spooning it out whenever anybody came up holding a pie tin. My trouble was that I didn't know what you had to do to get a pie tin. The smell of the stew was almost enough to make me go wild.

The guy with the spoon noticed me standing there but he didn't say anything at first. A little later he turned to me and said, "You look a little chucky, son." Chucky meant hungry.

"You are sure right about that," I said.

"All right," he said, "take my pan down to the creek and sand it out. Then bring it back and I'll load you up."

I went down to the creek and scoured the pan with sand, putting some elbow grease into it to make it shine. When I came back to the fire the guy gave me a pile of stew, adding a little extra splash of gravy at the end. Oh, man, I never tasted anything so fucking gorgeous in all my life. I felt so good when I was through that I almost set my plate and spoon down on the ground without going to the creek to clean them. That was one of the rules: wash up the minute you finished eating. You could take any pie tin or cup off a nail at any time and know that they were clean.

The guy with the spoon took a little liking to me, and offered to show me a few things. "Know what kind of country this is?" he asked me. "This is mosquito country. Ever bed down in mosquito country?"

When he mentioned bedding down my guard went up. I thought he might be trying to play position on me. Not that there were a lot of queers in the jungles. Oh, sometimes an old guy would want to take care of a young guy, but not too often. Once I almost climbed into a boxcar without noticing that over in the corner were two white guys and a black guy, one cornholing another while the second guy was blowing the third, I forget in which order. A regular love triangle. I backed out in a hurry; I didn't want to join that party. That sort of stuff has never appealed to me.

The guy in the Colton jungle was no threat; he wanted to help me, and he did. He took out a pocketknife and started cutting small branches off the eucalyptus trees. "Eucalyptus and mosquitoes don't go together, you know," he said. I didn't know, but I learned.

He made a pile of crisscrossed branches about five feet high. Not crisscrossed any old way, but in a special way. It took him about forty minutes, even though he worked fast and knew what he was doing. "Don't just climb in," he said when he was done. "You've got to take a running leap and land right in the top of the pile. That way you break into the middle and the branches close around you."

He had to coax me, because I thought it might be some kind of joke. For all I knew, the bums would bust out laughing if I jumped on that pile and bang their spoons on their pans. But nothing like that happened. I made a running jump, a swan dive, onto the top. I didn't even hit bottom; I just sank down as soft as a feather into the middle, and the branches closed around me, like he said.

I slept like a baby.

11
Life
at
the
Bottom

To get from Los Angeles to San Francisco I didn't have to hop a freight. I was standing on the corner of Ninth and Main in Los Angeles asking some skid-row bums to point out the cheapest flop in town when a car pulled up. Ooga, ooga, ooga. I looked up and there was a great big sonofabitch behind the wheel, waving for me to come over. I pointed at myself and said, "Me?" "Yes, you." I walked over thinking, Jesus, now what.

"Know anybody going to San Francisco?" the guy said. It was the biggest coincidence of my life. When I told him I was headed there he asked me if I was in any particular hurry. "It'll take five or six days," he said, "but you'll get your room and board. All you will have to do is drive my car part of the way."

It was a deal. I thought it would be a breeze, but it turned out to be one of the dirtiest things I have ever been involved in. That bastard was repossessing cars. He had a list of everybody between

Los Angeles and San Francisco who had missed three payments. He needed me to drive his car back to the nearest garage when he put the snatch on one. After a day or two he said he would pay me something if I would snatch the cars and let him drive his own, but I said fuck that shit, I don't want buckshot in *my* ass.

At night we would end up in Bakersfield, Fresno, Modesto, places like that. He would stay in the best hotel and give me fifty cents for a flop, but I would spend only half of that and use the rest for alcohol and hustling. I made a few bucks hustling. In Los Banos I went into a place that had nothing but Mexican pea-pickers in it. They broke their backs all day in the hot sun, but did I feel sorry for them? Hell, no. I stayed in that joint playing pool till I had every cent there was to be had, which was a little over nineteen dollars. When I was hanging up my cue they started talking among themselves and nodding toward me. I began to get a little worried, but I made a move that may have saved my skin. I sent a guy out to get a gallon of wine. We passed that jug back and forth for half an hour, and when everybody seemed to be in a better mood, I eased out the front door and sprinted to my flophouse.

The car stealer dropped me off in Oakland at one-thirty in the morning. I hopped on the tailgate of a truck that was waiting for the ferry and rode across the bay to San Francisco. San Francisco! I had made it at last. It was too late to phone anybody, so I decided I would just find a cheap bed for the night and get some sleep. It was a beautiful night, and I felt wonderful. You know, a song in my heart.

I hopped off the truck at the Ferry Building and started stepping down Market Street. Then I saw the cop, a cop who had spent a lifetime waiting for me to come on the scene. He stood in the middle of the sidewalk, fists on his hips, rocking back and forth, heel and toe, waiting for me to get to him.

Now instead of trying to slip past him as if I was guilty of something, I took a different tack, and it really irritated him. Before he could say anything to me, I raised my hand and said, "Excuse me, officer, could you by any chance tell me where I might secure a cheap lodging?"

He came right back at me, talking in a thick brogue: "Cud I till ye where ye cud git a cheap lodgin'? Why, ye goddam bum, git your ass up the street before I kick it clear up on your shoulders. Git over to skid row and stay there." He must have been about to grab me by the shirt when I gave him the big hello, and it made him mad.

I found a fleabag on Third Street and slept till noon. I called my uncle and my mother and made a date to meet them at a restaurant for dinner. Then I shaved, sharpening my straight razor on the mirror. To do that you put some soap on the glass and rub the razor on it in little circles—an old hobo trick. The edge won't stay on very long, but it gets sharp enough to slit your throat, which is what I felt like doing after dinner.

I suppose that day was a pretty important one in my life, now that I think about it, but it is very dim. All I remember is how I felt when it was over. What I expected of my mother and uncle, I don't know. There was no job I could imagine that I wanted, even if they had one to offer me. But I had gone through such hell to get to San Francisco! I thought I was coming back home, that it would be like a family reunion. Well, Jesus Christ, she wasn't even glad to see me. Why should she have been? She had gotten nothing but trouble from me, and my aunts had no doubt told her that I had gone from bad to worse. She knew I was a drunk and a bum, so there was no goddam reason she should have been glad to see me.

We made small talk for awhile, until they got fidgety and made it plain that they wanted to get back to whatever they were doing when I busted in on them. I walked out of that restaurant in a daze. I could hardly wait to get out of town. I didn't realize it at the time, but right then was when I really did become a drunk and a bum and a two-bit hustler. I was already, in a way, but up to then I had a temporary feeling about it—I always thought that by next Tuesday I would straighten myself out and settle down. But when my mother and my uncle gave me the cold treatment, I thought to myself, "What's the use?" For the next few years I bounced around the country like a yo-yo. I lived the low life. I didn't give a shit what happened to me. I went without food for days. I slept in ditches.

Here is the kind of thing I would do. *Four times* I went into whorehouses flat broke and diddled the best-looking hooker in the joint, which is pretty stupid when there is an eight-foot pimp hanging around. Twice when I got my pants back on I just flew out the front door—Fleet-footed Dan—and raced for the railroad yard, jumping on the first freight going in any direction. Nobody was ever peppy enough to chase me and catch me. And, you know, a pimp can't very well run down the street hollering: "Stop that man! I'm a pimp and he stiffed my whore!"

The other two times I pretended I forgot my wallet. "It's in my other pants at the hotel," I would say, as if I had a hotel and another pair of pants.

I learned a lot of things in those years. I learned how to roll a cigarette on top of a boxcar doing sixty miles an hour, which takes a steady hand and a lot of practice.

I learned how to keep a fire going on the floor of a boxcar without burning the thing apart. Lighting a fire on railroad property was a penitentiary offense.

I learned how to ride the rods. Under every railroad car are steel rods running from one end to the other. You didn't just hang onto them like an acrobat, you laid boards over them, crosswise. If you were good you did your platform work after the train was under way. Even with a good platform, it paid to tie yourself on with your belt, and to blindfold yourself with your handkerchief—otherwise you got blinded by the sand and grit that shot in your face. Even tied on, it was dangerous to fall asleep, because you were inches from certain death. Once I actually pissed my pants when I nodded off and woke up losing my balance. Yes, you can nod off under a railroad car, even though there is a terrific roar and a constant clickety-clickety-click.

I found out the hard way that on the Texas Pacific you better have at least a quart of water with you, because that baby doesn't stop clear across that fucking state.

I saw some things, too. I saw a family of nine riding a freight. At every stop the hobos stole fruit and vegetables for them. Even the brakemen on the train helped. Nobody was allowed to ride closer than two cars from that family, because there were a couple of teen-age girls they wanted to protect. Oh, we took good care of that family.

I saw guys go goofy on a drink made from milk and natural gas. Some of the cheap hotel rooms in those days had gas jets on the walls that still worked. Guys would turn the jets facing the floor and make the gas bubble through a quart of milk, which they would drink. I've seen guys high on that stuff running along the tops of trains doing sixty miles an hour, laughing and jumping from one car to another like Fred Astaire and Ginger Rogers. When they came to a flatcar they stopped just in time. The Lord takes care of fools and drunks.

So many people as bad off as I was, that's the reason I was able to keep going. Plus I could play pool. I always had a little hope in me because of that, always felt that maybe in the next town I would get lucky—get the mayor in a game and win the deed to the county courthouse or something.

Some towns were tough. Reno was tough. If you couldn't show the cops some money they would take you to the edge of town, point to the mountains, and say, "Start walking." Fort Bragg, California, was tough. I got there by passenger train. People tell me, "Oh, that is such a nice trip up the coast to Fort Bragg." Like hell it is, not when you are hanging onto the back end of a caboose while the conductor is pounding on your fingers with a stick.

In Fort Bragg I used to lay in wait in the pool hall for the loggers to come in on payday. One day the cops showed up first. They dropped me at the city limits. "Get lost," they said.

The railroad bulls were terrible. I saw one walk past two white guys on top of a boxcar and try to throw a black man over the side. This was while the train was sailing down the track. Well, it turned out that the bull was the one who got thrown off, and not over the side, either—down between the cars.

Cheyenne Red was one famous railroad bull I was lucky enough to never meet. He had a reputation all over the country for being the absolute worst. His favorite trick was to ride a train about forty miles out of Cheyenne and stop it in the middle of the desert, miles from water. That's where he threw everybody off.

The boys finally caught up with him, too.

I made some good scores hustling, but when I did I got drunk on the money. I would stroll into the poolroom in a jerkwater town and ask the desk man to get me a game for all the money I had on me. "How good do you play?" "I'll tell you," I would say, "I can beat all the assholes around here." "You can?" That usually got me a game right away. The game was always pool. You never saw billiard tables except in the big cities.

I took some odd jobs—I had to. I pearl dived—washed dishes. I picked crap off trees. On menial jobs, Jesus Christ, they expected you to break your ass and then pay you nothing.

I picked high-pole hops near Ukiah, California, in the hot sun. I mean the temperature was over a hundred. There was an Indian squaw who was a little warm for me, and she gave me a bag in the morning with about twenty-five pounds already in it. You think that's a lot? They were paying a penny a pound, and it took about three hours of hard work to pick that much. When you brought your sack to the truck for weighing there better not be too many leaves or twigs in it, because they dumped it out on the road and made you start over.

Sometimes if it was cold and the jail wasn't full, the cops let you spend a night in a cell, but usually they said, "Are you kidding? Get the hell out of here, we're not running a hotel."

The more I bummed around, the more I missed my wife. Even Chicago began to seem like a good place to be—at least I knew my way around there. So I drifted back there and moved in with my wife. I tried to find a job. Me and ten million other guys. My wife couldn't understand how a person as brilliant as I was couldn't get a fine position. She thought I should be president of Standard Oil of Illinois, at least.

She didn't like my friends. She would see me walking down the street with one of my pals and later she would say, "How can you stand a man like that? How can you even be seen on the street with him? He looks like he is going to stick somebody up any minute."

"You mean Bad Eye? Why, how can you say such a thing?"

I wasn't back in Chicago more than a month when I'll be a sonofabitch if I wasn't rounded up again by the cops for some gangland murder. By my own cousins, Burt and Jim.

"My God," I said, "you know I didn't do it . . ."

"We don't know nothing, Dan. We haven't seen you for a long time. How do we know what you've been doing? You better come along with us."

That did it for me as far as Chicago was concerned. As soon as I got out of the bucket I decided to go back to San Francisco, which was the other town I knew well. This time I would ignore my mother and my uncle. My wife didn't want me to go, but I couldn't help that. I told her again that I would send for her. It had been nice seeing her, but it would be just as nice getting away from her. She was so good, so understanding and decent, that she was driving me nuts. So away I went again, riding freights to the west.

I really did intend to send for my wife eventually, but I never seemed to get around to it, and after a year or two of waiting she divorced me. I forget on what grounds. "Aggravated inattention," I think it was. I knew I forced her to do it, but that didn't make me feel any better.

12

Getting Through the Thirties

Pool halls were crowded during the Depression. The more people lost their jobs, the more people there were to hang around. The customers didn't have much money, but there were a lot of them. *Pool Hall Burns Down—5,000 men homeless.* That was a common joke, but it wasn't funny.

Graney had died in 1927, but his Billiard Academy was still one of the best rooms in the country, with carpets, fancy woodwork, stained-glass chandeliers, beautiful equipment. He had thirty-six tables, twenty-two of them billiards. I was hired to brush the billiard tables in Graney's probably six different times during the Depression. I did a good job. I even ran my handkerchief through the little hole in the corners to get the dust completely off the cloth.

Graney's was the action room—that's where the money was changing hands. Graney himself was a sporting man, involved in all kinds of sports, and he liked to see action. The story is that he paid off the cops every week so they wouldn't bother him about the gambling that went on in the joint. One old guy told me that he was sitting in Graney's during the twenties when two rookie cops wandered in. Graney saw them and jumped off his stool behind the counter. "Did somebody send for you guys?" he said. The cops shrugged and said no. "Good-by, then," Graney said. "When I want you I'll call you." The cops turned around and left.

The other big room in San Francisco was Wright's, on Ellis Street. There were twenty-four tables on the main floor, sixteen of them billiards, and four snookers on the balcony. Chick Wright ran the place with an iron hand and only let people in whose looks he liked, which made it something like a private club. When you walked up the long flight of stairs to Wright's you were met by a man at the top who was, shall we say, impeccably attired. If he didn't care for your appearance his first words were, "Something you wanted?" That was Chick Wright himself, with his high-button shoes. You better have a suit and tie on, or you could forget about playing there. You could flash a roll of bills and say, "Why, I could buy this whole fucking joint, you old sonofabitch," and he would say, "I'd rather you bought the place down the street."

I remember a sea captain named Elmore Hawkins who walked up those stairs wearing a $250 suede jacket that was so fancy and well made that it would cost $1,000 today. But Chick didn't like it, and he stopped him. Hawkins pulled out $3,000 in cash and said, "You mean my money's no good here?" "Your money is welcome," Chick said, "it's you we don't want." Can you imagine that happening today?

It was Graney's I headed for when I got to San Francisco the second time. I had eight dollars in my pocket, and I didn't have a place to stay. I was well dressed and fairly clean.

"I'd like to play a game of three-cushion," I said to the house man.

"How good do you play?"

"Listen," I said, "you can trot out your best, and I don't want to play for fun."

The guy was not impressed. "Well," he said, "we do have a player here who wants a game, but he is pretty good."

"Bring him on, because I am pretty fucking good myself."

We went over to table number seventeen, way over by the phone booths, and I played this guy 25 points for two dollars. I rained billiards, winning 25–11. I was young then, and didn't know how tough some of those shots were. I did notice, though, that when we started playing, all the sweaters—the spectators, the ones who just sit and sweat—moved over to watch our game. One of them was an old bastard with a hawkshaw pipe who kept talking to himself. Not loud, but I could hear him. "Holy Christ," he said, "who is this kid, anyway? No kid ever beat Joe like that. What do you think about that! A kid walks in off the street and beats Joe."

In the second game I shot out to about 10–5, but by that time the old guy was getting on my nerves and I needed a drink. I finally went over to him and said, "Look, fella, I respect your age and what have you, but I am getting tired of you whispering about the guy I am playing. Who is he?"

"You really want to know?"

"Yes, I really want to know. Who the hell is he?"

"It's Joe Hall. He's the new world's amateur champion."

When I heard the words "world's champion" I was through. I don't care if it is in horseshoes, "world's champion" always impresses the hell out of me. I only made three more points. I couldn't hit the end rail. Thank God I had sense enough to quit playing him for money.

Word got around town fast that I won a game from Joe Hall,

which finished me as a hustler in San Francisco. After that I had to go to Stockton, Tracy, Reno, Fresno, even Salt Lake City to get games. But San Francisco was like home to me, so I stayed there most of the time, taking jobs in pool halls when I had to.

Times were awful tough. Guys were sleeping five or six in a two-bit room. One guy would rent the room and the rest would sit in the lobby waiting for the clerk to go to the pisser so they could run up the stairs.

In a restaurant you could get three eggs and all the toast you could eat for a dime, if you had a dime. People would sit at lunch counters all day if they could. Prop up a newspaper and go sound asleep sitting there. Then the cops would come in, pick them up, and drop them at the edge of town. That was the easiest thing for the city to do—let some other place worry about the bums.

Plenty of times I didn't have enough money for a flop. I used to sneak into hotels and try all the doors, hoping to find an open room where I could sack out. Sometimes I would walk into the Dale Talac Hotel, where I knew the night clerk.

"How you doing, Blackie, old boy?" I would say.

"Danny! Say, you're looking pretty sharp tonight."

He knew why I was there, but he would dummy up. I ran errands for him now and then, like getting a bottle of booze up to room so-and-so. I waited around till a broad walked in with a trick. They might register as Mr. and Mrs. Ipshitz, with no luggage. What I counted on is that they wouldn't fuck all night, that they would get tired of it after an hour or so and come back down the stairs. That's when I would race up to the room. Blackie looked the other way; he didn't mind, because the room was already paid for. I would turn the sheets over and sleep till check-out time.

When I worked in pool halls I always hated closing the place, because it meant I had to wake guys up and throw them out. Old men, and some not so old, would file out into the cold with faces a mile long, some of them with swollen feet because they hadn't had their shoes off in weeks. But I had to do it, otherwise I would get fired and not be able to afford a place to sleep myself.

I worked in Fresno for Thurmond Jack. Nobody remembers him now, but at one time he was the greatest rotation player alive.

I worked at the Crawford Bar in Bakersfield, owned by George Helm, who parted his white hair in the middle like a billy goat, and who was my friend until he died.

I worked at a billiard parlor called the Rialto in San Francisco, wearing an apron with coin pockets in it. My job was to collect two-and-a-half cents a cue from the snooker players when they started a new game. Olson, the manager, sewed the pockets of my pants shut at the start of each shift so I would have to put the money in the apron. A few months of that and I began to get the idea that he didn't trust me.

I got quite a surprise one night. I was in Salt Lake City trying to beat some poor sonofabitch out of his lunch money, when a squad car pulled up in front of the joint I was in and two cops strolled through the front door. "You got a guy in here by the name of McGoorty?"

I laid my cue on the table and walked calmly to the back of the room and out the back door. Once outside I turned on the speed. There was another cop there in the dark, and Fleetfooted Dan ran right into his arms.

"Where you going, Mr. McGoorty?" he said.

"I don't know who fingered me," I said, "but he's a lying sonofabitch. I've been in that poolroom all night and all day. And all last night, too. I haven't even been down to the corner to buy a paper."

"Take it easy," the copper said. "We don't want you for anything. We have a message for you."

I thought I knew what the message would be: "See those mountains? Start walking." But that wasn't it.

"Your mother died yesterday. They want you in San Francisco."

That uncle of mine, he had found out from some of my friends that I was probably hustling in Salt Lake City and he phoned the cops to canvass the pool halls. But a message was all he sent. No money for a train ticket. So I had to hop freights and goose the ghost—we never said "hitchhike"; it was always "goose the ghost."

By the time I got to San Francisco my mother was buried. I felt awful bad about it—a beautiful woman like that dying so young. If I had seen her on her death bed I probably would have tried to make up with her, or apologize. I was never much of a joy to her.

My uncle had me sign some papers. I didn't read them, and I have no doubt now that I was given a royal screwing. If my mother had anything when she died, there wasn't anything left for me. There was no estate at all, my uncle told me. Soon as I signed those papers he took off for Tonopah, Nevada, and I never saw him again.

My mother left me just one thing: a bill for two thousand bucks at St. Mary's Hospital. That's how much they charged her for dying of cancer. I was the son and heir and closest relative, so the bill was made out to me. They kept mailing that bill to me, month after month. "Some mail for you, Dan," clerks at fleabags here and there would say to me. And it would be that fucking bill. The hospital didn't realize how ridiculous it was. They couldn't imagine that a man of my age, as well dressed as I was, was worth only thirty-seven cents in cash. My only asset was a twenty-ounce cue.

Finally I went out to the hospital and had a talk with the Chief Collector, or whatever he was.

"Listen," I said to him, "you are billing me for something I didn't order. You kept my mother alive for two months with glass tubes. You didn't ask me if you should do that. I didn't even know about it. I didn't even know she was sick. I was in Salt Lake City, for chrissakes."

"You are morally and legally obligated to pay."

"I want to tell you something. You can't squeeze blood out of a turnip." I wasn't trying to be brilliant; I was just trying to get through.

"We understand your grief." It was a year after the funeral, and he was understanding my grief. "But a hospital is a business, too. We tried our best to save your mother and to make her last hours comfortable, and if you ever get any money we will tie it up."

"Thank you very much."

As it turned out, I did get hold of some money later, but I didn't tell St. Mary's about it. During World War II I had $10,681 at one time. It's been thirty-seven years since my mother died, and the bill still has not been paid.

I lived in Sacramento for a year or so. At one time I had a pretty big cleaning and dyeing route. My truck quite often had a thousand dollars' worth of pajamas, bathrobes, towels, and trick suits in it, because most of my main customers were whorehouses. I had almost every one. The cops put me out of business by nailing me for drunken driving and taking away my chauffeur's license.

Sacramento was quite an open town, more so than San Francisco. There were whorehouses all along J Street and K Street. One place, Helen's, guaranteed no broads older than sixteen— the most beautiful young snatch you ever saw in your life. There were cheaper places on L, M, N, and O, including the "window tap" joints. You are walking along the sidewalk and you hear a tap at a window. When you round, you see a broad with her elbow on the sill saying, "Hello, sweetheart." The cost was between a dollar and two dollars, but you could bargain with them. I was sitting in a parked car one night when a hooker tapped on the windshield and said, "Want to have some fun?"

"Sure," I said, "what did you have in mind?"

"Got a couple of bucks?"

Turned out that she climbed in beside me and copped my joint for forty-five cents. I didn't even want my joint copped, but I wanted to see how much she would cut her price. The topper is that my friend Tom Ward was sitting in the back seat the whole time. The broad didn't pay any attention to him; he could have been Cardinal Spellman for all she cared. Ward razzed me for years afterward. "That cheap goddam McGoorty," he would say to crowds of people, "he made that poor girl blow his wazzle for a lousy forty-five cents, telling her that's all he had, when I know for a fact that he had a ten-dollar bill pinned to his undershirt."

There were some very fancy houses in San Francisco, like Sally Stanford's. Most of the tricks there were turned by appointment, but you could walk in the front door cold if you were well dressed and they had some idea of who you were. I bluffed my way in a couple of times just to get a free hard-on. I sat in the plush parlor in an overstuffed chair like a big spender and looked at all the girls. "Is this all the girls you got? What else are you hiding in the back?" And they would trot out a few more. The girls wore nothing but a thin veil and maybe a flap over each tit. They sat right on your lap and tried to get you steamed up. When I got all the kicks I could I walked out as if I didn't see anything I wanted. Then they wouldn't let me in any more.

For quite a while I worked in the Bercut-Richards cannery in Sacramento for two bits an hour. My job was to roll in crates of peaches and dump them on a moving belt, where they were grabbed and sorted out by a string of broads. One day the owner of the Union Billiard Room downtown heard that Johnny Layton, the world's three-cushion champ, was going to be in town that night and available for an exhibition. "Who the hell can we throw against him?" was the question. And somebody said, "There is only one player in town who would stand a chance. He's working out at Bercut-Richards."

About noon my boss, Archie Donabedian, came out on the platform above me and said, "Hey, you . . ."

"Yeah?"

"Do you play billiards?"

"A little."

"Johnny Layton is in town, just for tonight. They want you to play him."

"Oh, Jesus Christ," I said, "I'm not in shape . . . I've been wrestling these crates of peaches and I need a drink and I don't feel so good."

"You can have the afternoon off to practice."

"For Layton? That's not enough time."

Archie climbed down off the platform and put his arm around my shoulder. "I want you to play him, kid. And I want you to win. I want you to win for Bercut-Richards."

I had played Layton an exhibition game once before, in Chicago in 1927. He beat my brains out, but he was nice about it. He was a hell of a swell guy. I also played with him a few times in those seven-point games in the back room at Kieckhefer's, in the days when I was cutting my teeth on the best players in the world. So Layton recognized me when he saw me. He gave me a nice hello, but I know he figured I was just another pushover.

I remember every point in the game. He jumped out to a 14–2 lead, but then he got the "nearies," just barely missing shot after shot. That gave me hope, boosted my confidence, and I started raining billiards. It was a 50-point game, and I remember when the score was 42–41 in his favor. He ran a four. I played him safe. One and duck. One, one, one. The score was 49–48 in his favor when I made a five-cushion bank. I studied the balls and all I could see for the game point was a force-follow around the table. I had to follow through to miss a kiss, and then get my speed and angle off the third rail. The ivory balls we were using were beautiful, and they would follow like a dream if you stroked them right. The cueball would hold the English on the third and fourth rails instead of dying out after two rails the way composition balls do today. I looked the shot over real good, and figured that instead of a return off the second diamond I would have to come off about three-fourths, with maximum English. I hit the ball hard, and when it jumped off the third rail and started crawling down the table you could hear a pin drop in the joint. You would have sworn that cueball was going to stop, but it kept coming, and when it hit the fourth rail it spurted to one side to count off the other ball. A big cheer went up, as you can imagine. That win brought me a ten-dollar bill, a jug of wine, and an all-night drinking bout with Johnny.

A month later I played him another exhibition in San Francisco and beat him again. That's when he said I had a hex on him. "For years I've heard about the Indian Sign," he said, "but I never believed it. You have convinced me." So we went out and got drunk. Johnny Layton's face was always flushed and red, because he drank too much. It didn't bother him though, and it didn't kill him the way it did quite a few others. He was a wonderful player, and I was lucky to get those wins over him. "Mr. Solid," we used to call him because of his grip and stance. His bridge, the way he held the cue on the table with his left hand, was absolutely firm and secure. It would have taken three firemen with pickaxes to tear it apart.

When I beat Layton the second time I got another big cheer, but not like in Sacramento. I have never been very well liked in San Francisco, maybe because of my arrogance, my vulgarity, my way of not giving a shit what I said. I believed what some young broad told me once—that I was pretty cute.

I played some good billiards in the thirties. Playing for fun against Con Buckley, who needed a spot of 25 points in 50, I got my lifetime high run of 21. I tell that to very few people, because when I do they think I am pouring piss in their ears. A run of 21 in three-cushion billiards is so phenomenal that you practically need affidavits from the spectators.

In 1934 I entered the San Francisco Bay Counties tournament. I finished second, but I got my all-time high tournament run: 15. That may not sound like much, but the high-run record for a world's tournament is still only 17. I am not a high-run type of player because I play too much defense. In the National in 1964 I ran back-to-back nines against Bill Hynes, and if I had missed any one of those 18 points he would have had shit to shoot at.

Finishing second in 1934 and first in 1935 had quite an effect on my life. For one thing, I never had to pay table time again, not anywhere, for the rest of my life. Room owners like to have tournament winners hanging around and playing—they figure it is good for business, so they don't charge them. For another thing, people started asking me for lessons. Teaching billiards, which I think I am pretty good at, has kept me from starving to death.

One of the best players I had to beat out to win the 1935 tournament was the Seattle Kid. He was very slow and methodical, so slow they thought about barring him. He would stand at the table and chalk his cue in extreme slow motion. One day I played him ten 25-point games for two dollars a game, and that bastard ran nine four times. That is something—four nines in one day playing short games. I would be knocking on the door, needing two or three points, and he would step up and run nine and out. "I guess I just know when to make my move," he would say. He would say things like that that ate you right up.

This is no lie: I'll bet that in my lifetime no less than fifty different people have asked me, "Why do they call him the Seattle Kid?" Jesus Christ, who is buried in Grant's Tomb? Imagine just getting slaughtered by him and some old fart comes up behind you and says, "I wonder why they call him the Seattle Kid?" You feel like turning around with your cue and butting him to death. "Because he's from Poughkeepsie," I would always say.

The Seattle Kid. His real name was Arthur Kreshell. He made a big chart showing the cueball paths and returns for the diamond system. You still see blueprints of that chart hanging in various rooms, with no credit to him.

In the thirties I think I won the majority of the local tournaments in San Francisco, plus a few in Los Angeles. Typical for me was that I would draw money out of the prize fund as the thing went along, so that when the tournament was over I would have about thirty cents coming, even though I might have won $150.

God, how I needed that money. It was so hard to get. People had no place to sleep, no place to eat. There was no such thing as welfare, and you couldn't hang your head and go over to St. Boniface's for a free meal like you can today.

The guy who saved my life and helped me last until World War II came to the rescue was Verne Littlefield, who owned two billiard rooms and a livery service for marriages and funerals. He gave me jobs when I was desperate. One was to go to Los Angeles and look for bargains in used limousines. When I found one he sent me the money to buy it and drive it back. Did I have fun hustling in those big cars! I stayed in top hotels; right at Hollywood and Vine. I could spit out the window and hit the Pantages Theater. It is amazing to think what a ten-dollar bill was worth in those days. At a classy hotel a ten-dollar bill got you a corner room with bath. For a week.

Littlefield liked to go on hustling trips with me, as my backer. He liked the action. I might be hung over, and he would say, "Come on, Dan, let's take a trip and make a little money."

"Jesus, Verne, I don't know . . . I'm a little shaky . . ."

"Aw, you'll be all right when you have a few snorts under your belt."

Finally World War II started, and not a minute too soon. Right away everything changed for the better. For hustlers, Pearl Harbor was like pennies from heaven.

In 1948, Danny McGoorty surprised the billiard world by staying sober long enough to win the Pacific Coast three-cushion billiard tournament over a very strong field. His following second-place finish in the United States National in Chicago motivated him to become an ex-pool hustler and, several years later, an ex-drunk.

A pensive McGoorty chats with Romie Yanez at the latter's billiard room at 401 South Main in Los Angeles, circa 1950. Yanez can be seen demonstrating geometry by shooting billiard shots on a Disney educational film called *Donald Duck in Math Magicland* (1959), now available on videotape.

The legendary Willie Hoppe at age twenty-two in 1910. He won his first billiard world championship in Paris at the age of eighteen in 1906 and his last in San Francisco in 1952, a span of years unprecedented in any game or sport. "It is as necessary to control your emotions," Hoppe said, "as it is the balls." At the world tournament in 1948, a *Chicago Tribune* headline read: "Hoppe lowers the boom, so down goes McGoorty."

Augie Kieckhefer won four national titles, the last in 1932. He owned a fifty-five-table room in Chicago at 18 East Randolph Street as well as a thriving billiard chalk company he inherited from his father. According to McGoorty, he lost it all on uncooperative horses.

Jay Bozeman was born in Vallejo, California, in 1906 and died there ninety years later. He was one of the best players in history never to win the world championship, finishing second a frustrating five times. His style, flair, and accuracy made McGoorty sick to his stomach.

One of the few players ever to win world titles in both pool and billiards was a stumpy, red-faced Irishman named Johnny Layton, of Sedalia, Missouri. McGoorty got drunk with him many times and twice beat him in exhibition games. Mr. Solid, he was called because of his bridge and stance. "His bridge," McGoorty recalled, "the way he wrapped his fingers around the cue on the table, was so firm and secure it would have taken three firemen with pickaxes to tear it apart."

The stylish, charismatic Ralph Greenleaf, who dominated pool from 1919 to 1938, is one of many great players who ruined his career with alcohol. Here he zeros in on a practice shot before a match with the doomed Charles "Chick" Seaback, jokingly called the greatest player in the world of Lebanese descent. People loved hats in those days. Greenleaf once toured the nation with a vaudeville troupe shooting trick shots onstage with an angled mirror over the table so the audience could see what he was doing.

McGoorty and a few of his friends at the bar of Jay Bozeman's billiard room in Vallejo, California, in the late 1940s. Left to right are many-times world champion Welker Cochran, 1953 world champion Ray Kilgore, five-times world runner-up Jay Bozeman, Dan McGoorty, and Tex Zimmerman, owner of a billiard supply store in San Francisco.

The two Willies pose with their world championship trophies after the 1951 tournament. Mosconi, left, almost unbeatable at pool in his prime, was also an excellent billiards player. Hoppe was moderately good at pool, but spent his long career focused on billiards, which is played on a pocketless table. He stayed fit, didn't drink or smoke, and didn't even go to movies for fear it would tire his eyes.

Welker Cochran, right, was so amazed at the prowess of Japan's Masako Katsura that he came out of retirement to play her a series of exhibition games in California, which he just barely won. Katsura's best game was straight billiards, at which she once ran 10,000 points. McGoorty said that you couldn't ease up on her because she was a woman or she would take the balls and "stick them right up your pooper." He managed to split their ten matches.

One of McGoorty's many short-lived jobs was house pro at a poolroom in San Francisco that hired models as waitresses. Dan called it the best job he ever had. "I got ten bucks a day per broad."

McGoorty's last hurrah was in the 1966 world invitational tournament in San Francisco. Past his prime at age sixty-five, he played well, but not well enough to contend for the title. "I was thrown off my game," he said, "by the politeness and good sportsmanship of the foreign players."

The best black billiards player by far in the 1960s was Chicago's Richard "Baby Brother" Powell. This wonderfully atmospheric scene, captured by an unknown photographer, comes courtesy of James Parker, owner of the Illinois Billiard Club in Willow Run, Illinois.

After fifteen years of obscurity, Masako Katsura was persuaded to give a five-minute demonstration at a tournament in San Francisco in 1976. Despite not having touched a cue in ten years, she easily ran a hundred points in straight billiards. She was ambidextrous and, according to McGoorty, "flipped the cue from hand to hand like a chopstick."

Alfredo De Oro was a master at whipping out a handkerchief, striking a match, or sneezing just as his opponent was about to hit the cueball. He was seventy-one years old when this photo was taken during the 1936 world tournament, when he pulled off one of his cleverest hustles. He managed to win his game with the powerful Welker Cochran by not asking for a bathroom break. Cochran became so worried about the old man's bladder that he couldn't concentrate on the game.

13

The World War II Festival

In 1940 nothing was happening. Hustlers used to wait in line in the rooms, day after day, hoping a mark would walk in. Sometimes they were reduced to hustling each other. The rooms were full of guys flat broke, out of work, staring into space. I started going into YMCA's, hoping to find somebody, anybody, willing to play a game for a nickel or a dime. Then, when the shooting started overseas, things began changing for the better . . . slow at first, then faster and faster.

Guys started showing up with money in their pockets. Then a few more. Then before you knew it everybody had jobs, and new people were showing up everywhere with all kinds of money to spend. Holy Christ, by 1942 I was surrounded by marks and saps and suckers of all descriptions. They were pouring into California from all over, cashing checks right and left, looking for people to lose their money to.

World War II was like spending four years with your hands in other people's pockets. World War II was a field day, a thieves' paradise, a . . . festival.

I mean, here were guys wanting to play five- and ten-dollar nine-ball who didn't know which end of the cue to use—that's how ridiculous it was. I hung around joints in Port Chicago, Benecia, Richmond, all the shipping-off points. The kids in the service were waiting to be sent to fight Japan. They figured they were going to get killed, so they didn't care about money at all. They would even share their cookies from home with us while we were robbing them.

We would make up all kinds of games to get them started playing. "You make the one-ball in the side pocket, and I'll make fifty balls in the other five pockets." That sounds like a terrific handicap, but it really isn't; you just make sure you never leave the guy a decent shot at the one in the side. If he gets his ball close to the hole you just knock it away. But it sounded good—fifty balls to his one. I can still hear a sailor moaning to his buddies as he forked over his money: "Ah cain't onnerstan how he can make all those balls in all those pockets and ah cain't make the goddam one in the sad."

All kinds of con games went on. "Listen, soldier, I can have a girl in the alley in ten minutes, but she won't come unless I give her the money first, see?" So the soldier pays the money and runs into the alley, where he waits with his pants at half-mast. Naturally, the pimp goes south with the money.

I didn't indulge in that kind of con. I had a very good reputation when it came to things of that sort. Guys like Tugboat, why, he would beat a kid out of a one-cent popsicle. In those days he was a total hustler, which is to say a total thief. But he was way above Behind-the-Back Leon, or Morgan, The One-Armed Bandit. Tugboat was an angel compared to them.

We all made money. You couldn't help it. You couldn't trip over a curbing without some guy in the gutter saying, "Okay, you win. Here's your ten bucks." Even the sergeants in the PX's got doublesmart and started cutting themselves in, getting a piece of the action instead of protecting the troops. They would tell us who could play and who couldn't, and make sure nobody bothered us while the money games were under way. I guess they figured the kids were going to lose their money anyway, or were going to get killed overseas, so they might as well stick their own oars in and get what they could.

I used to like to walk up to a table where two soldiers were playing each other and ask if they cared to make it three-handed. They would look at each other and figure they had a lock, figure they could sandwich me. One would leave me tough and the other would leave setups for his partner. You could almost hear them wink. It is an extra pleasure to beat guys like that, who think they are hustling you.

I tried Los Angeles during the war, taking jobs during the day and hustling at night. Labor was in awful short supply and the jobs paid too well to refuse. I managed the big poolroom in the Alexandria Hotel, tended bar, worked in an aircraft plant. Everybody was desperate for help. I got married again, to a woman who had a good job, and we rented a very nice place on LaSalle Street. We were both bringing home the bacon. That was when I counted up the cash on hand and found $10,681. It was the best I ever lived. We were farting against silk.

For a few months I was so busy, holding down three jobs at once, trying to make a killing while I could, that I didn't have time to drink. My poor wife, she thought I had gone on the wagon, and she actually got a little color in her cheeks.

Then the war ended. The jobs dried up, the soldiers and sailors disappeared, my wife and I drifted apart, and I lost quite a bit on horses and boxers. It was fun while it lasted.

14

Into
the
Big Time

In the fall of 1947 I was tending bar at the Trojan Recreation in Los Angeles. The phone rang. It was a guy named Robinson, who was sponsoring a three-cushion tournament. "Danny," he said, "I wish you would get in this thing and show these guys how to play billiards."

"Well, Robby, it's nice of you to say that, but I haven't played a game of billiards in six years." It was true. I had been playing nothing but pool and snooker with our fighting men. In 1947 everybody was still walking around wearing fatigues to prove they had been in the service.

This guy Robinson was very high on my game. He thought I was a great player. He meant it, too—he wasn't just blowing smoke up my ass. He kept after me, kept telling me that I could get back in shape in a week if I wanted to. I finally told him I would come over to his joint and see if I could still hit a ball.

He had nineteen brand new tables. I threw a set of ivories out and started batting them around. I had no feel at all. Nothing seemed right. Then some guy came in, I don't remember who, and I played him a game. About halfway through my touch started coming back. Things started coming back to me . . .

A whole series of tournaments had been set up, ending with a chance at Willie Hoppe for the world title. First there were city tournaments, which is what Robinson was putting on, then there were sectional tournaments, and then a National at Navy Pier in Chicago with all the sectional winners. The top three finishers in that would advance to a double round robin with Hoppe. What the hell, I thought to myself, as I watched the balls rolling around in Robinson's place, I might as well try for it.

I won the city with a record of six wins and one loss. The next step was tougher—the Pacific Coast Sectional, with city champs from all over the West, but there was a long wait, which gave me plenty of time to get my game back. Only the winner would advance to Chicago, so I knew it would be a very hard-fought competition. I did my best to control my drinking, and managed to cut it down to just a few beers in the evening, followed by a sandwich to soak it up and a glass of milk before hitting the sack.

I won the Sectional, too, playing probably the best billiards in my life. In the final play-offs against Joe Procita, John Fitzpatrick, and Ray Kilgore I averaged .99999, which made a few eyeballs pop. I even got a telegram from Hoppe himself: "Is this the Dan McGoorty I used to know?" He was always very proper—called me Dan instead of Danny. Or Prick.

My game against Fitzpatrick was a cliff-hanger. As usual, he cried and complained and begged and leaned and scratched and clawed and ran twelves and thirteens. He was awful hard to beat. I needed one point, I remember, when I left him a shot that had a kiss in it. There were several ways for him to play it, but the most tempting was the one with the kiss. I closed my eyes and prayed that he would go for it, that he wouldn't change his mind and play safe. He went for it. He took the chance. Now anybody who has seen Fitzpatrick play knows that his favorite kind of body English is a jump in the air. He puts his feet together and hops one way or the other. When he got the kiss he went straight up for about forty feet, turning red and white and almost putting a hole in the ceiling with his head.

In the last game I beat Kilgore, who won the world title a few years later, 50–44 in forty-six innings. He called me a liar: "Nobody can lay off for six years and play that good. It don't make sense. You must have a table in your basement."

Shit, I didn't even have a basement.

There I was, the first player from the coast to play his way into the National in years and years. Cochran and Bozeman had been seeded in many times, sure, but I was the first one to play his way in. Nobody could believe it. I could hardly believe it myself. I knew I could play, yes, but I didn't know exactly how good. I had never been in a major tournament before.

One guy, George Hardt was his name, came up to me and said, "I never heard of anything so ridiculous in all my life. You? Going to Chicago to play against Hoppe, Chamaco, and Navarra?"

"Listen, you prick," I said, "I am going back there whether you like it or not." I had won $300, along with the plane ticket.

"No, no, don't get me wrong . . . I admire you for having so much goddam guts."

"That makes it worse, you fucking skunk." Oh, how I wanted to poke him in the nose. He was just my size, too—four foot three and seventy-nine years old.

But I got a lot of encouragement. Christ, I got telegrams and post cards from all over the country, from hoodlums I had forgotten all about. Gus Copulus encouraged me—a man I idolized when he played in the old Interstate League. He was through as a serious player because of back trouble, but he could still shoot the shit out of them balls. I've seen him wearing a brace, can't even bend over, walking stiffly around the table, running eleven, fourteen, twelve, Jesus Christ. He was born in '95.

There was another long wait before the National in Chicago, and I got nervous as a caged tiger. When the date got closer I couldn't stand it, and went back two weeks early.

Players got nine dollars a day subsistence. If I could have I would have slept in doorways to make a little extra money, but they were doing the thing up first class and had me booked into the Congress Hotel. My room alone was nine dollars a day. It was so big I could have rented it out for dime dances.

I got a hell of a reception from all of my so-called friends in Chicago; a lot of them I hadn't seen in twenty years. One pick-pocket I knew was now a big sportswriter. He arranged to have the porters at the hotel make me carry my own luggage when I checked in while he took my picture, which he ran in the paper with some smart caption. "Chicago is proud of you, Danny," I think it was.

All the hoods came around. "How much did it cost you to buy your way into this tournament?" "You must be a pimp to be able to play billiards all the time." Stuff like that I got. I was the only qualifier from the coast—there was no number fucking two man—and they couldn't get over it.

But plenty of my old friends came around who wished me well and meant it. They hadn't seen me for twenty years, and here I was, coming back to town to appear in the Big Show. There was old Charley Brush, there was Tommy Cleary and Marty Malaney. Shamrock Eakin was there, and so was Scarface Foreaker. Scarface was tickled to death for me.

I made up my mind to do my absolute best, not because there was two thousand bucks for first and a thousand for second, but because it was a way for me to more or less justify my existence, to shut up my critics. Oh, man, I had plenty of critics, people who let me know one way or another that billiards was the only thing in life I was worth a shit at. I had to do well. I fought a running battle every day to stay away from the bottle. During the tournament I did not take one drink.

The competition was awful tough. Joe Chamaco of Mexico was defending champion. Juan Navarra was champion of South America; Miguel Márquez, champion of Mexico. There was Sol Lurie, who won the Chicago sectional, and there was Eartrumpet Davis, who was hard of hearing and had one of the ugliest wives I ever saw. There was Lou Elkan and Tiff Denton and Jean Albert. Albert was from Venezuela and invited me to come down there and play because I was nice to him and didn't try to roust him. Some guys make fun of foreigners, kid around with them and embarrass them, but I never did that. If a guy doesn't speak English too good I leave him alone or try to help him out. It's too much work to try to roust a foreigner. Christ sake, call him a dirty bastard and he's liable to smile and give you change for a quarter.

Players came to town from all over to see the action and to stir some up for themselves after hours. I saw The Eufala Kid and Johnny Irish, two of the greatest pool players in the world, and they didn't have carfare to get out to Navy Pier. I took them out myself on opening day and got Annie Oakleys for them to get in.

Johnny Irish—I remember when I first saw him. It was during the war, in some dump or other. He was on a stool leaning back against the wall with his hat down over his eyes. I didn't notice him at first, thought he was asleep. Somebody said, "That fucking Churchill, he sure stands up to them krauts, don't he?" "Yeah," somebody else said, "he's got a lot of guts." That's when Johnny Irish spoke up. He didn't move a muscle, he just said, "Churchill? Can he run a hundred balls?"

Johnny Irish never played in tournaments. They made him nervous. He tried it once and got so nervous he was called for a foul the first time he walked up to the table. "Foul? What the hell for?" So the referee told him: "Because you are chalking your cue with the three-ball."

The 1949 National Three-Cushion Championship* was part of the Chicago Boat and Outdoor Show. It was a big commercial fair, but there was all kinds of activities—fly casting, duck calling, archery, every goddam thing. It cost $1.25 to get into the Pier, and after you walked a mile out to the end it cost another 85 cents to get into the billiard arena. It was a beautiful setup for a tournament, with steep bleachers all around and a good view from every seat. Even if Wilt Chamberlain was sitting in front of you you wouldn't have to say, "Hey, bud, a little to the left."

A three-cushion and a straight-pool tournament ran at the same time. There were nine tables lined up end to end, every other one billiards. Mixing the pool and billiard players together like that was crazy, and was the idea of the Assistant Scorekeeper, who was a woman. She didn't know much about running a tournament, but she was a hell of a lay . . . one of the best I ever had. The fact that she was Assistant Scorekeeper probably meant that the Chief Scorekeeper was getting the red part in too, but that is just a guess.

I was hoping I wouldn't have to open the show, but no such luck. I think every tournament I have ever been in I have had to open the damned thing, which I hate because of all the ceremony. Here you haven't slept all night worrying about the game and then you have to put up with all the picture taking and speeches. And the introduction of the players! "Ladies and gentlemen, it is my pleasure to introduce to you, on table number one, two of the outstanding dark horses of the game: Mr. Alfonzo Sneeze and Mr. Floyd Ipshitz. When Mr. Ipshitz was twelve years old he played his first game of three-cushion and ran eighteen."

---

*A tournament well covered by the press. *Chicago Tribune* files show that McGoorty's billiard memory was amazingly detailed and accurate. —RB

Not only did I have to open the tournament, I had to play Chamaco. I knew Chamaco. Did I know him! He is one of the few people in the world who owes me money. He came up to Los Angeles once in a while to have a good time, just the way people go down to Tijuana to have a good time. Joe almost missed the tournament. He overslept on the plane and wound up in Cleveland. He made it back to Chicago just in time, running into a meeting of players and officials and saying, "Deed I mees ze banquet?" When he heard that he played me in the opening game he said, "He play pussy good, but I play pussy good, too." Everything was "pussy good" with him.

Two hours before the opening game I was at the Illinois Athletic Club practicing while all my friends were trying to get me to take a drink. I got so nervous I had to put down my cue and walk back and forth in a hallway like a lion in a zoo. Willie Hoppe was sitting on a sofa watching me, holding his cigarette holder in that aloof way he had. I had known him for twenty-five years, but I was by no means a close friend. He was always very gentlemanly and he never gave advice, but he gave me some then and it helped quite a bit.

"Sit down, Dan," he said. "You look a little nervous."

"Look a little nervous! I'm as nervous as a hoor in church."

"Let me remind you of something. You earned the right to be here. People have to pay to see you play. As far as the other players are concerned, you play better than most of them. You will win your share of games."

Having him talk like that was quite an honor. I went out to the pier feeling as good as could be expected.

First thing I heard when I got there was that the odds were six to one against me. That didn't help me any. And nobody could get any money down on me even at those odds. One creep trying to get a line on how bad Chamaco would beat me sneaked up to me and whispered, "How many points do you think you will get, Danny?" How do you like that? Right before the game!

"I'm going to get to fifty before he does, you stupid cock-sucker," I said.

As I put my cue together I saw a couple of things that gave me hope. One was that there was Simonis Number One cloth on the tables. It was the first year since the war that they were able to get cloth from Belgium. I hoped Joe wouldn't remember as well as I did what it was like. Joe was used to the burlap put out by Brunswick.

The other thing was that the pool players on each side of us were quiet types. It is impossible for me to play well next to a nervous, fidgety character who looks like he might shit or go blind at any minute.

Taking my warm-up shots I noticed the big swing on crosstable shots. The cueball took a big dip instead of going straight across the way it does on the cloth they have in most places today. Unless you are playing on Simonis Super Roulante, which is like Simonis Number One used to be. Simonis Number One today is shit.

I won the lag, and when I hit the break shot Joe jumped out of his seat, thinking I had killed the cueball and would come in at least half a diamond short. But the ball came off the third rail nice and long and I scored right in the face, dropping the red into the far corner for an easy second shot.

I got off to an early lead, and it kept getting bigger, even though Joe started hustling me a little. "Thees goddam keed," I would hear him say while I was stroking, "he takes too long to shoots." But unless somebody in the audience is really riding me I have pretty good concentration. I won the game 50–37 in sixty-six innings.

Soon as it was over, and it was a very big upset, headlines in the Trib the next day, Joe said to me, "What took you so long? Come on, let's go get drink."

"Fuck you," I said, "I ain't gonna get no drink."

"You no going to buy me drink?"

"I'll buy you drinks till they come out your ears, but none for me."

Joe never lost another game. He went through the rest of the players like they were back-pedaling. He had a big stroke . . . too big, really. He always had to hold himself back.

Right away I lost three games to much inferior players, Elkan, Albert, and Eartrumpet Davis. Eartrumpet hustled me something awful. Every time I bent down to shoot, just as I was about to pull the trigger, he made his wife jump up in my line of sight and go out for coffee.

Then I started winning, but my game against Márquez almost made me a nervous wreck for life. The referee did his best to beat me. I had to make the game billiard three times before he would give it to me. Three times I made it, and right in front of two of the greatest pairs of eyes in the world in the person of Willie Mosconi and Jimmy Caras. You know how you can just barely tickle a ball? Especially an ivory on a heavy nap. That bugger will wiggle, but don't blink your eyes or you ain't gonna see it move.

"I didn't see it move," said the ref.

"He made it," said Mosconi, which he had no business doing. He was not the referee, he was sitting in the press box. Which is another thing—he had no business sitting in the press box.

But the ref didn't see it, so I didn't get it. A few minutes later I tickled it again.

"No billiard. Nothing for Mr. McGoorty."

I was flabbergasted. I looked over at Caras, sitting at the side, and he was pumping his head up and down, and the whole audience was whispering, "He made the fucking shot." But it did no good.

I went back to my seat really hot. The ref walked by and said, "For Christ sakes, Danny, he needs twelve . . . what are you so excited about?"

What am I so excited about? All afternoon at the Athletic Club this guy Márquez was running seventeens, nineteens, eighteens . . . Holy Christ.

I finally made the game point so square they could see it out in Aurora, but I squawked so much about that referee that he didn't work another game.

Solly Lurie tried to upset me, too, but it didn't work. I was ahead 28–21, and when I came back to the player's seat after a shot he stood up and said, "Tell you what. I'll bet you ten bucks I win. And I'll bet another ten you've made a bum bet." He had heard I was always broke, so he was trying to put the pressure on.

I took the bet, and even though he started shooting the lights out he couldn't overtake my lead. Playing for money has never bothered me. Tournament games are much harder than money games because you never get a second chance.

My final two games were cliff-hangers. I beat Tiff Denton 50–49 in sixty-two innings and Navarra 50–47 in fifty-eight innings. So I finished second behind Chamaco and ahead of Navarra. The three of us started a double round robin the next day with Hoppe for the world title.

I mentioned that the odds against my beating Chamaco were six to one. The odds were set mainly by Butch the Horticulturalist. Now Butch the Horticulturalist was the kind of oddsmaker who was not above trying to influence the outcome of a game after the bets were in. One night Butch started to ride Willie Mosconi, who was defending his world pool crown. Butch must have laid some big money on Willie losing. I was playing about three tables away, so I heard everything.

"Why you punk Dago," Butch hollered from the stands, "you can't play. You're nothing but a mama's boy. What kind of face powder do you use?" Trying to break Mosconi down, which he did, finally.

There was a brass railing around the area where the tables

were. Mosconi walked over to the rail, looked up into the audience, and said, "Butch, you no-good, dirty sonofabitch, I ought to let you have it with this cue."

"Go on, throw it," Butch said, "I'm short of kindling." Oh, Butch really gave him the harassmus.

McElligott stepped in then and put a stop to it. He was the chief referee, and a good one. He never allowed anything or anybody to get out of hand during a tournament, and in this case he was backed up by the sponsor, the Tribune, which was practically like the Chicago Police Department.

"Shut up, Butch," McElligott said.

"I paid my way in," Butch said.

"I don't care if you paid three ways in, you are a nuisance, and if you make one more crack I'll have you arrested."

That's how McElligott operated. Mr. Referee, we called him. Butch shut up and Willie won his game. Mosconi, I have to say, was the greatest pool player of all time, much as I admired Ralph Greenleaf.

Guess who I had to play in the opening game of the World's? Right. Hoppe. And not only did I have to play Hoppe, I had to play him when he was at the absolute top of his game. He was about to set an all-time record for a professional tournament of 1.33 points per inning. He was terrific . . . not sensational, but always in complete control of the game. It seemed like every time I stepped to the table my ball was frozen to the gum and the other two balls were out of sight at the other end.

Any daydreams I had of being world champion were taken care of that first game. Hoppe murdered me 50–20 in thirty-one innings. The Tribune headline was: HOPPE LOWERS THE BOOM, SO DOWN GOES MCGOORTY. Then Chamaco broke my heart 50–49. Navarra did it to me 50–43. I could have used about a week off at that point to pull myself together, but I had to go right back against Hoppe. I played the toughest defense I knew how, but I couldn't stop him from scoring. He scored in nine innings in a row at one point. He won 50–39.

I went into something like a state of shock. I overlooked shots. I fired and fell back without bearing down. I finished the tournament without winning a game, which I think is a record for a world competition. And, oh, were my so-called friends telling me what to do! I must have had five thousand coaches from Chicago alone. Did they crucify me while I was losing game after game! "You shanty Irishman!" they would holler. "You fucking donkey! You shouldn't have been allowed to play in the first place." That is hard to take when you are sitting in the player's chair trying to concentrate. It eats into you. Eats. Eats. I could have complained to McElligott, but then everybody would have screamed, "Crybaby! Crybaby!"

Those days were hell. I think I would have jumped off the Tribune Tower if it hadn't been for one thing: after every game I dragged myself back to the Congress Hotel and climbed into bed with the Assistant Scorekeeper. She saved my life.

Doing so lousy in that 1949 world tournament, not winning a single game, really sent me downhill. I got to drinking terribly. I got so I didn't care if I played billiards or not, the only thing in the world I could do better than the next man. I was fed up with the game and with myself.

Because I had finished second in the National, I had the right to enter the 1950 tournament, which I did without preparing my-self at all. I was a disgrace in that event, half drunk most of the time, out gallivanting around till all hours every night. Even so I finished fourth. One notch higher and I would have been in the World again.

Another lost year was 1951. I've heard people say that I used to crawl into Cochran's billiard room in San Francisco on my hands and knees, drunk, and they would have to throw me down the stairs to keep me out. I don't think I was ever that bad, but I do know that I was so drunk at times I couldn't remember what I did. Could be all the stories they tell about me are true.

I didn't pull out of it until 1952, when all the big players came to San Francisco for Hoppe's last tournament. Hoppe, Matsuyama, Kilgore, they all took me aside and told me what I was. They told me I was a no-good, lousy, useless drunk. So I surprised everybody again. I went on the wagon and never took another drink the rest of my days.

15

Beating
the
Bottle

The definition of a drunk is simple. If you are faced with a choice between breakfast and the giggle soup and you take the giggle soup, you are a drunk. I was in that category in the early twenties and I stayed in it for thirty years. I wasn't the type of drunk who hocked his old lady's jewelry and sold the baby's crib—I would just take whatever money I had at the time and go on a binge, and while I was sobering up I would have a few beers.

Part of my problem was that most of my friends and the people I most admired were drunks. I am thinking of Mr. Ralph Greenleaf. In 1922 Greenleaf was playing in the world's pool tournament at the Auditorium in Chicago. They had a beautiful amphitheater built up for the matches, really beautiful. Anybody who remembers the scene will say, "Why the fuck is it that they don't stage tournaments like that any more?" Well, he may not *say* it, but he will think it. About thirty minutes before one of Ralph's games he came busting into the men's shithouse looking like hell. I was always hanging around, so he knew me.

"Danny," he said, "you gotta get me a mickey. I need a mickey awful bad." A mickey was a flat pint.

"I will have to go all the way to Clark and Lake to get it, Ralph, and I don't know if I can make it in time, the weather the way it is."

"You'll make it . . . you've got to make it. Here's the money."

"I'm on my way."

"Don't let me down, kid." He called me "kid" even though he was only twenty-four himself at the time.

In heavy weather in the Loop cabs are no help, so I hustled both ways on foot through the snow and slush and shit. When I got back to the Auditorium I gave him the high sign and he followed me into the shithouse. He uncorked the bottle and, holy Christ, he started draining it. I grabbed his arm.

"Wait a minute," I said. "Not so fast."

"What's the matter? I need a drink . . ."

"You've had a drink. Worst thing you can do is to drink a whole mickey all at once. It might knock you out. Besides, I ran all the way . . . I need a drink . . ."

"Yeah, but you don't need it like I need it . . ."

"Listen, I need it. I'll keep the bottle. You'll get one break during the game. Meet me here then and take the rest." That's all the refs gave you in those days—one break during a game. They didn't care if you had diarrhea.

Knowing there was a bottle waiting for him was all Ralph needed. He went out under those lights and played the most beautiful pool you can imagine. A big five-by-ten table with small pockets, but he still got off a run of ninety. It was the greatest shooting I've ever seen.

Twenty-five years later he asked me again to get him a drink and I turned him down. I was managing the Alexandria Room in Los Angeles.

Ralph showed up for an exhibition sponsored by a thing called the Better Billiards Program. He was so loaded he could hardly talk, let alone play. He dragged himself around the table hanging onto the rails. It was so pitiful, so painful to watch that a lot of the spectators got up and left. I called the thing off, told the people Ralph was sick. I practically had to turn the lights out on him to make him stop.

"I'll be okay in a minute, Danny, I'll be okay in a minute."

"You will not be okay in a minute, Ralph. You are all through for tonight."

He was almost all through for good. Three years later, in 1950, he died at the age of fifty-one. Such a swell guy. Such a big talent.

Over and over again I saw what drinking could do to a man, how it could send the greatest of them right down the tubes, but I couldn't cut it out myself. I wanted to. I knew it was a bad deal. Hardly a night went by that I didn't sit on the edge of my bed, take one sock off, and tell myself that tomorrow I would smarten up and start making something of myself. Then I would put the sock back on, because I would get so nervous and anxious thinking about what a big effort I had to make to straighten myself out that I would have to have a little drink. That was the trap I was in. I couldn't face my problems without having a few drinks. Only when I was drinking did I have the courage to make up my mind to stop drinking. When I wasn't drinking, when I needed a drink, why, then it was impossible to think of anything but getting one.

When I needed a drink I had a frown on my face a mile deep and my mouth felt like it was full of cotton. If I had a few things to do that day it seemed like a few thousand. But when I got hold of some kind of drink, had that cold glass in my hand, then I calmed down. Relaxed. Tranquility. Like seeing the sun come out.

Many times I walked the streets at night wondering, worrying about how I was going to get a drink in the morning. If I was lucky I would run into some pineapple with a bottle who wanted to tell me his troubles. I always hoped he was in a really bad way, because the more troubles he had to tell me the more I would get to drink.

Sooner or later I would wind up in a room somewhere, sitting on the edge of a bed, taking off my clothes. When I got one sock off I would stop and stare at the floor. "I've got to get out of this town," I would say to myself. "Got to get away from this *environment* and all these losers." And a lot of times I would get out of town the next day, but wherever I landed I always seemed to run into the same kind of idiots I left behind.

One thing I never lost was my desire to be clean and to look good. I would shave every morning no matter how shaky I was. Sometimes it took a pint of whiskey to shave, to settle my nerves enough to shave. I didn't want to cut my throat by accident.

It was amazing, the good-looking starts I made in the morning after a bender. After the three S's—the shit, the shave, and the shower—I would put on a clean fiddle and an erky-dirk. Those are some of the old words. A fiddle and flute—that's a suit. The erky-dirk is the shirt. Lamb-fry is the tie. I was talking to a seventy-year-old man the other day who had never heard of anyone "carrying the banner." I could hardly believe it, because that was such a common expression back in the twenties and thirties. It means having no place to sleep. What I started out to say was that after a big blowout I always managed to put myself back together again. I would get all slicked up and walk out into the sunshine with a mouthful of Sen-sen. The Sen-sen didn't help me any—that was to help the other guy.

Most of the stupid things I have done in my life I can blame on the bellywash. Like the time Ray Mauer and I climbed on the coal car of the Seminole Limited bound for East St. Louis. We would never have done a thing like that if we hadn't spent the day in a schoolyard drinking home brew out of a washtub.

I got to be fairly well known in most of the big towns as some kind of a player, which meant that there were usually people who would take me out to dinner and buy me a few drinks till I could make a small score. I never knew who was going to recognize me. Once in San Francisco I was picked up and thrown in jail for being on the wrong side of Market Street. Vagged. If you were on the north side of the street broke you got vagged, because that's where all the nice stores were. Of course, I was drunk, too. I wound up in the San Francisco Bastille between Washington and Clay streets on Kearny. The Graystone Hotel, we called it.

Coming out of the drunk tank in the morning I was sent up to see the jail doctor, whose job it was to make sure the drunks were sober enough to go out on their own and get drunk again. "Well," he said to me with a smile, "how do you think you'll be hitting the ball today?" Jesus Christ, he was one of the sweaters who watched me play all the time. I got to know that particular croaker pretty well. Even got him to prescribe whiskey for me. That was the only way to get it legally during Prohibition. Getting a jail doc to prescribe booze for me, for "medicinal" purposes, was one of my finest works of art. I sure got a lot of sideways looks from druggists.

My drinking got awful bad. I would drink anything. Panther Piss. Fusel oil. God, when I think of the poison I have poured into my stomach . . . I should have keeled over years ago. I am lucky to be here now with cancer. I have no license to moan about it, that's for sure, although I do it just the same.

Needing a drink was one thing, but needing a clean change of clothes, for me, was as bad. I got just as nervous about that as about drinking. There was a Chinese laundry in San Francisco I always went to. I knew all the help, knew when they stopped to eat. They ate in the back, all at a big table, chopsticks flying, and they got pretty pissed off at customers who came in and rang the bell at lunchtime. They made you wait. Something happened to me alongside that laundry that still makes me laugh when I think of it, although it wasn't funny to me at the time.

I needed my shirts, but I was broke, and the laundry wouldn't give me any more credit. I got so desperate I decided to dash in at lunchtime, grab my package, and run like a sonofabitch down the alley alongside the joint. I could make it easy, Fleet-footed Dan. Everybody knew how fast I was: If it was five minutes before post time at Bay Meadows race track, I could run from Graney's Billiard Academy across four Market Street trolley tracks and four bus lanes and be at Max's bookie joint at Sixth and Stevenson in time to place the bet. "Give it to McGoor," the boys would say. "That prick will make it with time to spare."

Right at lunchtime I flew into the Chinese laundry and grabbed my package off the shelf. The boys in the back dropped their chopsticks and looked at me as if I was nuts. I flew out the door, around the corner, and down the alley like I had robbed a bank. And what do you suppose I saw in front of me? Blocking the alley? All of those Chinese laundrymen, lined up waiting for me with knives and scissors and flatirons! They had shot out a side door. They grabbed me, but they let me go after taking the package back. "What happen to you?" they said. "You were good customer, but you no good boy now."

They were right.

For some reason, I just had to look decent. It gave me some pride. I didn't want people saying, "Look at that fucking Mc-Goorty with one orange sock and one green one. He must have slept in the gutter." No, I didn't want that. I wanted people to say, "Look at that fucking McGoorty; he looks like he just stepped out of a bandbox."

I hit my peak as a drunk in 1951 and 1952. I was not what you would call a "filthy" drunk, because I shaved and pressed my pants, but I would get out of line. Try to pick fights with Joe

Louis, stuff like that. A wise guy. But the drinking started getting to me. The 1952 World's Tournament in San Francisco gave me the push I needed to quit.

It was Hoppe's final tournament. Chamaco was in it, Masako Katsura, Crane, Bozeman, Kilgore . . . all friends of mine . . . Procita, Rubin, Matsuyama. Not me, though. Who wants a drunk in a tournament? They wouldn't even let me referee . . . at first. They put me on the scoreboard. By the end of the tournament, though, the referee they had brought in from Milwaukee had made so many mistakes they gave me the job for the last four games. Hoppe was a sick man in that tournament and sixty-five years old, but he still managed to come in first. It made him the oldest man in history to hold the world's championship in any sport.

Watching a tournament I might have been in, working the scoreboard instead of playing, having a dozen people tell me I was a stupid bastard for drinking instead of playing, it hurt, and it made me make up my mind once and for all to beat the bottle. One guy came up to me halfway through the tournament and told me that if I stayed sober for six months I could beat half the players with a cue stuck up my ass.

The day after the tournament ended my wife and I—I was married again and living in an apartment at Hyde and Ellis—threw a little shindig at our place for some of the players. It was a chance to relax and have a nice time. I had a few drinks, and then everybody in the place told me I was a no-good, lousy, useless drunken bum. No-good, lousy, fucking, useless drunken bum, I guess it was. Those were the last drinks I ever had.

The next day I told my wife I was going on the wagon, and I watched the color come into her cheeks. There was at least forty dollars' worth of whiskey in the apartment, most of it Chamaco's. He owes me money, but he did leave me with a lot of grog. I gave most of it away. I took a bottle downtown every day and gave it to somebody I had hoisted a few tiddlies with in years gone by.

No doctor took care of me, or anything like that. I sweated

it out cold. Oh, how I sweated it out! In bed all night sweating I. W. Harper out of one arm and Old Fitzgerald out of the other. Sometimes I got up and slept on the davenport so I wouldn't stink up my old lady. In the daytime I was surrounded by people downtown wanting me to take a little nip. Some very fine people didn't want me on the wagon. Sportswriters, jockeys, bookies, doctors, and lawyers, they all wanted me to have a little drink because, a few of them told me, I was "more entertaining" with a few under my belt. "Aw, come on, McGoorty, have a drink. What are you, a man or a mouse?" Those rotten cocksuckers.

The first ninety days were the hardest. I had heard that alcohol stays in your system for ninety days, that till that time has passed a yen for more will be there, and that's about how it was with me. I had some d.t.'s, some bad dreams. The only one I can remember that I had over and over was getting chased by a guy six stories tall while I had my foot stuck in a bucket. My foot was always stuck in a bucket. Just when he was about to grab me I would shout and wake myself up.

By June of 1952 I was in the clear. I was solidly on the wagon and I have never fallen off. Not even for a beer or a glass of wine. I was surprised at how much will power I had. A lifetime drunk and I beat the bottle completely on my own, cold turkey, with only my wife to help me.

A few years later I quit smoking, too, which in a way was even harder. I lit up a cigarette one day and it tasted like the inside of an old motorman's glove, so I snuffed it out and never lit another.

Drinking seems so stupid to me now. When I see a guy boozing it up, a guy who could make something of himself, who doesn't know what he is getting into, it makes me sick. I have to walk away.

There is a foreign broad in the hotel where I have been living in the past few years who is quite a lush. Always trying to get the old men who sit around the lobby to buy her drinks. I bawled the hell out of her, finally. Some old guy had gotten his pension check and she was trying to get him started on the vinegar. I couldn't stand it.

"Why don't you stop that shit?" I said.

"What shit that?" she said.

"You know what shit I mean. You are trying to get that old man started on the wine. You know if he does he'll go hungry from the fifteenth to the first. But you don't care as long as he buys you a few drinks along the way. Just so you get *your* drinks out of it. You won't spend *your* money, though, oh, no, even though you have plenty and are on welfare and only fifty-four years old." Oh, I really gave it to her and she really needed it. When I was done all the old coots in the lobby stood up and gave me a round of applause.

I got in the elevator with that broad wagging her finger at me. "You should take drink yourself," she said. "You feel better. God says you supposed to drink. God says in Bible you supposed to drink."

"Listen, you leech," I said as the doors slid shut, "I don't know what Bible you've been reading, but if I were you I'd flush it down the pisser. And if you know what's good for you, you'll stay out of my way."

Which she did.

Part Three

●

A CAST
OF
CHARACTERS

●

• 16 •

From
Minnesota
Fats
to Big Alice

Minnesota Fats

I'm sorry, but Minnesota Fats was never a top player. He was good, sure, but not tops. There have always been at least twenty people in the country who would have been glad to swim a river of shit to play Fats for money. Fats won a lot of games and a lot of money in his life, but it was mainly because of the heavy hustle he used. Oh, the stream of bullshit he would pour on people was enough to make you sick. He was afraid to rely on his game alone; he had to constantly irritate the other guy. Either that or he would get his backers to put up so much money that his opponent would crack under the pressure. Even playing somebody like Zsa Zsa Gabor on his television show he was afraid of getting beat, wouldn't let her shoot in peace, kept bothering her and distracting her all the time. Now, if a man is afraid to play fair with Zsa Zsa, how do you think he would have done against real players like Wimpy Lassiter, Washington Rags, or even Big-Nose Roberts?

I suppose I shouldn't say these things, because Fats was always very nice to me. I heard him say once on a national hookup: "The only person left in the country who knows anything about three-cushion billiards is Danny McGoorty." But it is high time somebody stood up and said that Fats' estimate of his own ability is just part of his act. Why, his name is even made up. "Minnesota Fats" is just a nickname. His real name is New York Fats. He started using Minnesota because that's what the fat man was called in the movie *The Hustler.*

As a promotion man, that's different. He may very well be the all-time greatest promotion man, or con man. But a player? When he gets on television and says that he was the best, that everybody was afraid to play him, dozens of guys around the country jump out of their chairs and try to get to the toilet before they ruin the rug.

Greenleaf and Taberski

When I was learning to be a pool player, two of my idols were Ralph Greenleaf and Frank Taberski, who were trading the world championship back and forth. Greenleaf, young and stylish, was a great crowd favorite. He won most of the tournaments, but he always had a hell of a time beating Taberski. Taberski was a good-looking, impressive man, who looked like a distinguished lawyer. In fact, I think he was a distinguished lawyer at one time. When they played each other the joint was always packed.

Taberski squawked like hell about the way Greenleaf carried on during the game, making noise and moving around in his chair when Frank was trying to shoot, that sort of thing, but Greenleaf had plenty to squawk about himself. Taberski was one of the slowest players in the history of the world. One of their matches—125 points of rack pool—started at eight in the evening and was only half finished by 2:30. The few spectators that were left had to be woke up and told that the game was adjourned till the next night. It was because of Taberski that they decided to widen the tight pockets. Something had to be done to speed up the game or he would have killed it entirely.

I saw Taberski study a shot one night for forty minutes while Greenleaf sweated in his chair. It might have been only twenty minutes, but that is a long time to watch a man walking around a table studying a bunch of pool balls. I can remember the shot as plain as day. The cueball was in the center of the table and the balls were racked up with only two balls sticking out, one on each side near the top. He could make either ball but, no matter which one he picked, the shot would go nowhere because the other ball stopped him from breaking up the pack. I didn't know what he should have done, but an old-timer next to me smartened me up. "All he has to do," the guy said, "is split the two balls, kill the cueball, and drive both balls two rails behind the pack. Greenleaf will be locked up like a tied sheep."

Now get this. After twenty minutes of stalling, Taberski laid down his cue and went to the can! Can you imagine having that much gall? It wouldn't be allowed today. Today the referee would wait a few minutes and say, "Shoot or forfeit the inning." Or forfeit fifteen points, or the game. The referee has to keep things moving so the fans will be happy. But in the early days the ref didn't have that much authority. When Taberski got back from the can he announced a deliberate safety and shot the very shot the guy next to me said he should. Shooting a deliberate safety after all that stalling, well, it put the audience into such an uproar that they almost had to clear the auditorium.

Another time when those two were playing, Taberski got so mad at Ralph he socked him on the jaw and knocked him out. Usually Taberski was impossible to fluster. You could climb up on the table and shit right on the cloth and it wouldn't bother him. But this one night Greenleaf was doing every damned thing, talking while Frank was aiming, waving his handkerchief, spilling talcum powder on Frank's tuxedo, stepping on his shoes when they passed each other, and finally upsetting a glass of ice water on him. So Frank let him have it right on the jaw and got himself barred for a couple of years.

Greenleaf was a big talent. He pushed the high-run record on that tight equipment to 101 and then to 126. No telling what he might have done if he had stayed sober.

Bob Cannafax

There are a lot of ways to win without actually cheating, more ways in billiards than in most games because it is played in silence, with time between shots for studying and aiming. That gives the man in the chair a chance to sneeze, go to the can, knock over a chair, and so on. It is what is called the psychological hustle. In the plain ordinary hustle you hide your true speed; in the psychological hustle you try to drive your opponent out of his fucking skull. Make him nervous, at least.

There are many things you can do. Bob Cannafax, one of the great billiard players of the 1920's, used to pretend that something was wrong with his eyes. He squinted and blinked and seemed to be suffering. When he sat down in the player's chair after his inning he threw his head back and with a lot of showmanship put drops in his eyes, acting like he might go blind at any minute. The idea was to make it just a little harder for the other guy to concentrate on the game.

Cannafax had a wooden leg, and when he limped around the table he would slip a little and examine the floor and complain that there were some slick spots. That made the whole audience nervous, not just his opponent, because nobody wants to see a handicapped person fall on his ass.

Cannafax had a quick temper, too, and he made sure his opponent knew it. Once he was scheduled to play an exhibition game and a few hours beforehand he went to the room to look at the table. He didn't like the condition of the cloth and demanded that a new one be put on. The proprietor said he wouldn't do it. So Cannafax took out a penknife and ripped the cloth from one end to another. They had to change it, then. It was all part of his general hustle. When you played him you had to worry about his eyes, his leg, and his temper.

There is a small-time pool player in San Francisco called Snakeface who pretends that if he gets beat he might go crazy or get a heart attack. He's no youngster, but when he misses a shot or gets a bad break he jumps back, swings his cue in a circle, cusses with all his strength, and turns beet red. Years ago he used to put his head down and run himself into the wall, but he gave that up. This act puts quite a bit of pressure on the guy he is playing, who may not want to kill an old man for two dollars.

Alfredo De Oro

The all-time master of the psychological hustle was a Cuban: Alfredo De Oro. He was a foreigner, but he spoke fine English—not with a limp like so many of them. When I first saw him in 1920 he was already way over sixty years old, maybe over seventy. Because he had lost some of his skill he had learned every possible way to irritate the other fellow and throw him off his game.

In his time he was quite a player. The record book shows that he won the world's title in pool in 1887 and won it fifteen more times after that. He won the three-cushion title at least six times, back around the turn of the century.

I met a lot of the old-timers in 1923 when I won the Chicago Junior Amateur—Hoppe, Emmet Blankenship, Buffalo Dowd. Nobody ever heard of Buffalo Dowd today, but at one time he was one of the biggest thieves in the country. I played exhibitions against most of them—the young against the old.

In the 1920's De Oro was past his prime and getting hunch-backed. He couldn't shoot well anymore, but he won games with sheer orneriness. He was old, with a big soup-strainer mustache, but he wasn't feeble. You could tell he had played before, but you always knew in advance what shot he would shoot. He would go outside the first ball, dropping it against the end rail, and bring the cueball up to the other end near the red ball. Strictly run and hide. One and duck. Stall safeties. He averaged close to nothing but he never left anything to shoot at.

He complained constantly. He objected to the referee's calls. He went to the can and stayed there forever, but if the other guy took a quick piss he raised the roof and demanded the game by forfeit. He shot deliberate safeties and then argued that he had tried to score, walking around the arena looking into the audience for support. "Is there a man here who can honestly say I didn't try to make that shot?"

He was a rib artist with a million irritating remarks. If you ignored what he said to you, then he would mutter to himself on the sidelines. While his opponent was trying to shoot, Alfredo was polishing his cue, or chalking it with loud squeaks, or filing the tip, or dropping it on the floor, or coughing, or sending up clouds of talcum powder. If the referee told him to stop doing those things, he would start doing a whole raft of other things. I've seen him change shafts just for one shot, taking all day about it.

You see players today whipping out a handkerchief just when the man at the table is about to shoot, but you should have seen the way Alfredo did it. It was masterful. He kept his handkerchief folded like an accordion, with the tip sticking out so he could grab it without fumbling. It was big, a big brilliant white handkerchief. When he snaked it out of his pocket he always sort of shook it to the right and left like a long scarf before putting it to his nose and honking.

And the way he lit a cigar in the other guy's line of sight! His timing on striking the match was terrific. I used to sit in the stands trying to second-guess him. The man at the table would be stroking, just about ready to pull the trigger. Alfredo watched him like a hawk, holding a big kitchen match against a box ready to strike it. "Now!" I would think to myself, leaning forward, anticipating him, but he would wait. "Now!" Not yet. Alfredo waited, watching the man stroke, studying him, then suddenly he would strike the match just as the guy was bringing his cue forward to hit the cueball. It was beautiful.

He played defense at the table and offense on the sidelines, and the fans crowded in to watch his antics.

Once he managed to claw and scratch his way to win over Cochran in the days when Cochran could shoot the lights out. That crusty, bent old man won a game from the great Cochran, who was one of the flashiest, most brilliant players of all time. It was a sensation when it happened, and old-timers still talk about it. Cochran had an excuse, though, that has never been put in print before. He told it only to the members of his immediate family.

Here is what Welker said:

"I knew the old man would have to take at least six piss breaks during the game. I couldn't complain about it because of his age, and I wasn't going to let it bother me if he took a lot of time. Halfway through the game he hadn't yet asked for permission to leave the table, and I started worrying about him. Started worrying about his bladder. After an hour he still hadn't gone to the can. Was he all right? Was he going to go in his pants? Was he in pain trying to hold it back? I got so worried about his bladder I couldn't concentrate on what I was doing. That old man did not take one piss the whole game, and that is what beat me."

Willie Hoppe

Hoppe, Cochran, and Schaefer developed independently and were the three best players in the world for thirty-five years.

There was so much jealousy between them that it wound up a wonderful hate. Hoppe was very quiet about his hate, but not the other two. Schaefer was always hoping Cochran would say something to his face so he could belt him one in the nose.

The three of them stood out from all the other players, and the fans wanted to see them matched against each other, but it was hard for the promoters to get them together. They made it awful tough with demands for special conditions, even when the prize money was very good.

Hoppe reeked class. He never hustled his opponents in any obvious way. He was soft-spoken and reserved. Before a game he never walked around in front of the audience like Cannafax, shaking his fist and saying, "Dis bum won't get ten points." No, he would just walk out into the arena and stick the balls up the other guy's ass and not say a thing about it. I know—I've had 'em up there.

He was the cleanest-living billiard player in history. The only thing the other players had against him, besides his ability, was that he wouldn't lolligag with them and get drunk with them.

Hoppe is the only man who ever made a decent, steady living from playing billiards. He was on the Brunswick payroll for forty-seven years, and got other money from saying things like, "I use Monarch cushions because . . ." Cochran made money, but mainly as a room owner, although he did once beat a bootlegger out of $70,000 on a billiard table. But Hoppe, year in and year out, made a fine living his whole life just by being a player, with no gambling.

In my opinion he was the greatest all-around player of all time. Schaefer was a better balkline player, Cochran was a better shotmaker, but it was Hoppe who won most of the big tournaments. In an open game of three-cushion, with no deliberates allowed and optional cueball, I think both Cochran and Ceulemans would outscore Hoppe, but for total management of the game Hoppe was in a class by himself. He could take those three balls away from you and make you look like a fucking dummy, and it didn't take him three or four innings to do it, either. From 1936 to 1952, when he retired, he won eleven out of the fifteen three-cushion tournaments that he entered.

The greatest thing that has ever been done in three-cushion billiards he did in 1940–41. He came out of an oxygen tent and won twenty straight world tournament games, then the next year won fifteen more. A streak of thirty-five games in a row over the kind of competition he was up against is fantastic.

In Hoppe's book on how to play billiards is a long section on the diamond system, charts showing how to count the spots on the rails and figure out where to aim by using arithmetic. Now that is a joke, because he was not a system player. I went out to Navy Pier one morning during the 1950 tournament to practice and there was Hoppe all alone in the hall. He had the book open and was shooting shots from the diagrams . . . trying out the system. He looked up at me and said, "You know, Dan, it works. But you need a perfect stroke."

Those charts were put in the book by Byron Schoeman, and a lot of them are haywire. Sometimes one of my students will show me that book and say, "Look at this, McGoorty. Hoppe says you can hit the rail here and end up there."

"My boy," I say, "it can't be done. Those charts are just pretty pictures."

Not only did Hoppe not use the diamond system, he had nothing to do with developing it. That was done by Copulus, Layton, and Clarence Jackson.

Guys like Hoppe, Cochran, and Schaefer, they knew the table so well, all the angles, all the returns, they didn't need to use any system. They could get four out of two by elevating the cue a little and putting a touch of massé on the ball. The system? What system? Fuck the system.

Hoppe's biggest fault was second-guessing the referee . . .

hell, he first-guessed him. The least little questionable thing happened and he was out of his seat and you knew it was going to be a ten-minute hassle with all the tournament officials called in. Finally the verdict would be announced: "The committee rules in favor of Mr. Hoppe." Naturally. Who would have the nerve to disagree with the great Hoppe?

I would, and I did when I was refereeing the last few games of the 1952 tournament. The white ball was on the third diamond, the red ball was in a direct line with it and the opposite corner. He shot off the white and pretended to be trying to back out of the corner to hit the red. The shot just could not be made from that angle—there was no way. So I called him for shooting a deliberate safety, which meant that he couldn't shoot safe again on his next inning. He gave me a big look, but he sat down without a squawk because he knew I was right.

Later in the game I almost knocked him on his ass. He was shooting a double-the-rail shot, and when he pulled the trigger he tried to "coat" me . . . lean over the table and cut off my view with his coat. I'm not saying he did it on purpose, but I had to shove him out of the way to see the shot. He missed it by a hair. "No billiard for Mr. Hoppe," I called out. Then to him I said, "Sorry, Willie, but you had me blocked out." In his aloof way he said, "It is possible that you were standing in the wrong place." The hell with that—there was no place else to stand.

Hoppe used the upside-down bridge quite a lot, with the heel of his hand off the cloth. I don't approve of that because the hand is not quite as steady. That's a laugh, isn't it? My not approving of Hoppe's bridge?

I had nothing but admiration for the man. He was a true professional. Played every day. Took the game seriously. If he was in San Francisco and had to play an exhibition in New York, he would get off the train in Chicago and practice for a day or two before going on. He was known to do roadwork in the morning to stay in shape. Jogging. One morning he was running around a reservoir and met Cochran coming the other way. They didn't even say, "How do you do?"

They died within a few months of each other in 1959.

Welker Cochran

Not many people liked Welker Cochran, which seemed to be the way he wanted it. He was conceited, and he had reason to be. He was the greatest shooter the game has ever seen, a powerful offensive player. He first showed up, as far as I know, at the world balkline tournament in New York in 1919. He finished second behind Hoppe and ahead of Schaefer and had the high run of 265. A few years later he pushed the high-run record to 384, and then to 680. He won the balkline crown in 1927, his first of many titles.

When he and Hoppe took up three-cushion in the 1930's, every tournament went down to the wire with the two of them fighting it out for first. Only two or three times in the next twenty years did anybody else get the title away from them.

Cochran was the first of the big three to try for the three-cushion championship. In 1932 I was working at Graney's in San Francisco when Cochran came to town for the Pacific Coast Sectional. He had won the Los Angeles city tournament to qualify. A player of his caliber having to qualify in a city tournament! But those were the rules, and he had to start somewhere. In that meet he was something to see. He made shots that weren't in the book, shots nobody had ever seen before. He won with an average of 1.16, which was like breaking the four-minute mile. An average of more than 1.00 . . . nobody had ever reached that level before. At the Big Show the following month he came in first and averaged over 1.00 again. There he was, winner of the first world three-cushion tournament he ever entered.

What few people know is that Cochran was so busted at that time he borrowed a camel's hair coat from the Alhambra Flash to wear back to Chicago. I knew the Alhambra Flash well. I asked him, "What did Welker give you for the loan of your coat?"

"You know fucking well what he gave me," he said. "He never even thanked me. What's more, he kept it for a month afterward."

In the middle of the Depression Cochran, thanks to his world titles, was able to line up financial backing and bought out Graney's, which was going broke, with Dave Palm as a partner. Tough as times were, the two of them made a go of it, and they eventually made a lot of money out of the place, even though Welker had a terrible attitude for a room owner. His name was a big drawing card, but he was very unfriendly to the paying customers. Dave Palm's hard work put that operation in the black, in my opinion.

Here is the kind of thing Welker would do. He was walking toward his office one day past the billiard tables. I heard a good customer say, "Hey, Welker, how would you shoot this shot?" Welker kept right on going. "Welker," the guy said again, "look at this shot. How should I play it?"

As Welker opened the door to his office he turned his head a little and said, "If I showed you, you still couldn't make it." What a personality for a businessman! Poor Dave Palm; every time Welker drove somebody out he had to work to get somebody back.

Another thing about Cochran. Say he was shooting for the game point. The instant he saw the cueball take off in the right direction he walked back to the sidelines taking his cue apart. When the point was scoring he would have his back to the table, as much as to say, "Naturally the point will score and I will win. What did you expect?" And if the players were going to shake hands after the game, the other guy would have to come over to Welker . . . who would give him a limp fish. Welker would never go over to him.

What he loved to do was shoot force massé shots on brand

new cloths. The power he had! He brought his cue down so hard you thought it was going through the slate into the floor. He had one massé shot in particular he used to practice where the first object ball is about three feet away from the cueball, and all three balls are frozen to the rails. He made it quite often, and it was amazing to see the action on the cueball. Nobody else could come close to making it; nobody else could even get it started.

I hated Cochran and he hated me. In his opinion I was a disgrace to the game and should have been barred from everything. I know he kept me out of some tournaments I tried to get in. He loved the game, dedicated his life to it, didn't want anybody to detract from it.

Right after he won his first world three-cushion title, I played him an exhibition match. He didn't want to play, and you can't blame him. Beating me would prove nothing, and losing to me was a fate worse than death. But Dave Palm wanted to pep up business by pitting the new champ against the young upstart who had beat Layton twice not long before. Cochran finally agreed to play me one game.

In those days I was on the hustle all the time, morning to night, looking for a mark, looking for a drink, looking for a clean shirt for tomorrow. Here was another chance for me to attract a little attention, maybe get some pupils or something. I was gassed by game time, which irritated Cochran. I was hanging on the rails, and must have been a horror to watch, but I'll be goddammed if I didn't rain billiards. Everything I tried worked. I got kissed into points. I left him impossible shots by accident.

During the game the audience was rooting for me, because Cochran was disliked generally. Ernie Rodriguez was sitting behind the player's chair, and he whispered to me, "Give it to him, kid. Don't let him up, just keep giving it to him." I gave it to him and won 50–31.

When I made game point, here is what Cochran did. He said

in a voice loud enough for half the audience to hear, "Can you imagine this? I win the world's championship with the highest average ever scored, then I come home and lose to a no-good, drunken bum like him." It didn't help me any to hear that. Joe Hall was so mad I thought he was going to start swinging. I didn't want to fight, I wanted a drink, especially because they were free. Everybody wanted to set me up. Bozeman, with a smile from ear to ear, must have bought me forty dollars' worth of booze.

Cochran was always against me. Always. He didn't want to see me in any tournaments, even little room tournaments. Nothing. When the promoters insisted, saying they wanted all the best players, he would say, "But how can you even consider including a man who is an idiot drunk? Representing a game as beautiful as this?"

In a way, he was right. I have to admit that.

He hated me until 1953. When he saw I had quit drinking he changed a little. I guess it was my drinking that had been bothering him. I remember being in Los Angeles for the horses that year. A lot of people from San Francisco had gone down. I was staying at the St. Paul Hotel, with a toilet down the hall and a freeway interchange out the window. It was about noon, and the ponies had cleaned me out. My rent was paid, my bags were packed, and I didn't have so much as a quarter. Not a stick of gum, or a wet match. I had no way to get back to San Francisco and I didn't know what the hell I was going to do.

I was dressed and shaved, sitting on my suitcase staring at the wall, when the phone rang. I figured it would be the desk man. Desk men always know the minute you are broke. He was going to tell me that check-out time was at one o'clock and that there were people in the lobby waiting for my room and all that shit I've heard since I was a baby.

"Danny!" the voice on the phone said. It was Cochran, calling from the Statler. "I'm glad I caught you. I was just ready to start out for San Francisco in the car and wondered if you wanted to ride along. Have you thought about going back?"

I have been kissed into a lot of billiards in my life, but I've never been luckier than that. I don't know how I did it, but I said, "I suppose today is as good a day as any. Tell you what . . . I'll get packed and tie up some loose ends and meet you out in front in an hour."

"Good," he said. "I'll be there."

He even bought me a couple of meals on the drive north. While I studied the menu he would lean over and point to the cheapest thing on the list and say, "That looks like a good buy." Oh, he was tight.

As a person he was a tightwad and a cold fish, but as a player . . . then he was colorful, then he was a showman. If you were some palooka sitting in the bleachers at a tournament, Cochran was the guy you would watch. When the balls came to rest you wondered, "What will he do now?" You never knew what to expect. He was a fantastic shotmaker—a marvel.

In an open game he was better than Hoppe. That's not just my opinion, he proved it in a 5,400-point cross-country match in 1945. How they came to terms I'll never know, but they did. It was a match everybody was waiting for, the two big names in a showdown to settle all the arguments.

Cochran insisted on optional cueball on the first shot of each inning. The object was to please the fans and make some money, he said, and you can't do that with three-hour defensive struggles. He had a point, but another reason is that he didn't want to spend a month looking at Hoppe safeties. Hoppe used to safe him to death. Optional cueball means the game is all offense.

Hoppe got off to a big lead back east, but by the time they hit San Francisco for the final 300 points he was only 75 points ahead, which should have been enough. In front of the hometown fans Cochran caught fire, made everything, and won the match with a terrific rush at the end. Hoppe was so pissed he refused to shake hands. How do you like that? For the first time in his life Cochran offered to shake hands, and the other guy refused!

Jake Schaefer

Jake Schaefer had about as much personality as a doorknob. If a man lied all the time, or had a filthy mouth, at least he had a personality, but with Jake you didn't even have that. He was the greatest balkline player of all time, but he would have flopped as a night-club comedian. He was born in 1894 and is still in good shape, last I heard.

In 1931 Jake was sitting along the wall in Wright's Billiard Room in San Francisco talking to Herb Paul, one of the top horse handicappers in the country. Herb called me over to meet Jake.

"Here is a kid who can really play," Herb said to Jake. "You should see this kid play."

"I don't want to see any kids play," Jake said, not looking at me. "This game is going out, Mr. Paul." People called Herb Paul "Mr." because he was a topnotch handicapper.

Then Jake said to me, "Take up something else, kid." He went back to talking about Your Grandmother running three-eighths at Hollywood Park.

Not long after that I saw him again in Wright's. I said hello.

"Oh, you're the friend of Mr. Paul's," he said, in a much better mood. "Have a chair."

I sat down and we had a long talk. I talked about billiards and he talked about golf and horses. The only thing he said about billiards was that it was an idiot's game, that anybody could learn to be good at it who had nothing better to do. I talked to him every day for two years and not once did he show any interest in billiards.

Jake was the only world champion whose father was world champion before him, so he had solid coaching when he was a baby. The main advantage he had over other balkline players was his bridge; he could bridge up over anything for any kind of massé, even if the balls were clustered in the center of the table.

What soured him on the game, I think, was that balkline was dying out and that the promoters of tournaments wouldn't pay him enough. They would go $6,000, but he wanted $9,000. He was already getting more than Hoppe for appearing in balkline shows, but he didn't think it was enough. If this makes him sound money hungry, I'm sorry, because he wasn't. He just wanted to be well paid for what he did, and he deserved to be. He was a great artist. He figured that since he was the one the people came to see, the money should go to him and not to some promoter.

Jake detested the three-cushion tournaments because of the dinky prizes, but he would play exhibitions if the price was right. In about 1950 a series of five matches was set up between him and Cochran in California—in Modesto, Stockton, Bakersfield, Fresno, and Sacramento. Big posters were made up showing them full length, with a headline like "The Match of the Century." At the last minute Cochran backed out—I forget why. All I remember for sure is who they ran in as a substitute: Daniel John McGoorty, Pacific Coast Champion. Bozeman wasn't playing that year, and I was the best they could come up with on short notice. I didn't have to arrange for a leave of absence from my corporation or anything.

So I set out to play a man who had been my hero since I was in knickers. Each time we arrived at the joint where the game was, there was the big poster out front, with a black X painted across Cochran's face and name, and my name written in pencil somewhere down at the bottom. I found out on that tour that Jake was no cheapskate. He split the fees with me right down the middle. I told him it wasn't right. "It's okay," he said. "You probably need the money more than I do. Besides, you play better than I thought you did."

He didn't have much tact. In one town he walked up to the table we were going to use that night and said to the room owner, right in front of a bunch of his customers, "You mean we have to play on this shit?"

He was a wonderful talent, but deadly slow. He tried for perfection. He mapped out the shots in detail, putting his finger on the rail, staring at it for a minute, then moving it an eighth of an inch to the left. This might be on a simple shot that a drunken Girl Scout could make if you held her up to the table. What Jake was doing was calculating where all three balls would end up. He didn't just want them in general areas, he wanted them in certain exact spots. He wasn't just playing position for, say, a double-the-rail shot, he wanted a certain angle on the double-the-rail so that it would lead to a five-cushion shot afterward. Playing position, two, three shots in advance. I never saw Hoppe or Cochran do it.

Jake never gave me any lessons directly, never gave me any pointers—oh, he would have for three or four hundred dollars—but I learned a lot from playing against him. On cross-table shots, for instance, I noticed that he didn't often go to the end rail . . . he just went straight across, dipping just enough to make the count. His speed was perfect—when he missed, my ball would glide up to the other end of the table, clear up in Annie's room. Even when he took the speed off and my ball only went halfway up the table, I still would be looking at some goddam off-angle bank.

He poured the oil on me, left me absolutely nothing to shoot at. I tried to hate him, but I admired what he was doing to me. Sitting in the player's chair, it got to be almost funny to me, wondering what he would do to me next, wondering what I would find when I got to the table to take my turn. Would he leave my ball under the table?

Even so, even with his brilliant control of the game, people were walking out on us, because he was so slow. Measuring. Studying. I heard one guy stand up behind me and say, "Fuck this. I'll come back for the trick shots." One night at the hotel I got up enough nerve to mention to Jake that maybe we should speed the game up a little, that, after all, we were just trying to provide some entertainment. But he didn't care what the audience thought; he cared about the game and how it should be played. Here's how slow he was: In Fresno he made the fifty points in only thirty-eight innings, but the game took two hours and forty minutes.

I didn't win a single one of the five games we played, but I came close once. I need one point and I am looking at a big natural, a shot a chimpanzee can make, or an elephant with his trunk. I bend over, concentrate on it, and just as I am about to hit the ball the referee leans down and shouts as loud as he can in my ear: "Mr. McGoorty is shooting for the game point." Holy Christ, I jump a foot and miss the shot a mile.

I blew my stack at the guy, and even Jake bawled him out after running seven or nine or twelve, whatever he needed. "You shouldn't have interrupted Mr. McGoorty's stroke," Jake said.

"I wanted the crowd to know he only needed one," that fucking idiot said.

The worst part of the trip for me was that we played a hundred points of balkline before the three-cushion game. You can imagine how that turned out. I didn't get a single shot; he ran 100 and out every time. I didn't even get a break shot because when we lagged he always froze his ball on the rail. He would break, the balls would come together like trained pigs, and off he would go. Click, click, click. Every once in a while, just to let the fans know I was in the show, too, I would jump to my feet and wipe the sweat off my cue, but it didn't help any. Before we got to the three-cushion, where I had at least a chance of winning, Jake had my ego hammered down to the size of a pinhead.

One night I said to him, "Say, Jake, I think the audience would like it a little better if we played three-cushion first, then the balkline. What do you say?"

"No."

Jay Bozeman

The boys were talking about a young kid in Vallejo, California, who thought he was pretty good, so I scraped nineteen dollars together and got on a bus. Small town champs are usually good for a score because they can't chicken out of a money game without losing their position as local hero. Nobody from a burg like Vallejo, California, would be good enough to beat me, because that town is nowhere.

The young kid was Jay Bozeman. How he got so good living in the sticks I'll never know. I got off the bus and hung around the town joint till he came in—a tall, skinny redhead about twenty-two years old. I played him a few games for two dollars. I watched his style, his flair, his accuracy, and it made me sick to my stomach. He made everything he shot at! And he never hesitated a second—before the balls had come to a stop he had his hand on the table getting ready for the next shot. Sometimes he had a hard time waiting for the cueball to stop spinning. He had eyes in the back of his head and in his ass and everywhere. You never saw a guy run so many fives, sixes, eights, sevens . . . and when he missed, a look of amazement came over his face. It was no act— he was sincerely amazed when he missed.

I quit while I still had bus fare. That was in 1931, and for forty years I have been his biggest fan. He would have been world's champion if it hadn't been for his old lady—his first old lady, not the old lady he has now. The old lady he has now is the greatest.

When Cochran won the 1933 Pacific Coast Sectional, Bozeman was number two. At the World, Cochran was number one, Bozeman number two. From then until 1940 Bozeman was in every World, and he was always breathing all over Cochran and Hoppe, he was right on their asses, and if he hadn't quit playing during the war years he would have taken the title at least once.

After the war he tried a couple of more times. In Hoppe's last tournament, in 1952, Bozeman would have tied for first if he had beaten Ray Kilgore. He had already won one game in only twenty-three innings, tying a record he set himself in 1940. But I'll be a sonofabitch if Ray didn't knock him in the creek, dropping him into a second place tie with Matsuyama. Jay was so mad he went into a bar on Ellis Street and broke all five of his cues. He swore off the game forever.

The next year he decided to try one more time. Hoppe was through, so the thing figured to be won by Jay. Now when you finish second time after time it begins to eat into you. Some people say that Bozeman was a great player but that he always dogged it when the chips were down. How can you say that a man who finished second to Cochran and Hoppe was dogging it? Only one can win, and if Bozeman had tried a few more times it would have been him. I know he can play under pressure; I've seen him play too many money games.

The 1953 tournament—which was the last big professional meet ever held—came down to the wire with Bozeman and Kilgore tied with 7–2 records. Bozeman was a big favorite in the final game against Kilgore. It was Bozeman's turn to be champion, everybody thought. But when he walked into the arena I knew he was going to lose—the expression on his face: he looked like a dog shitting peach pits. Kilgore won and it was second place for Jay again. He hung up his cue for good.

In 1966 he almost came out of retirement to play in a world amateur tournament. The new players—Ceulemans of Belgium, Ogata of Japan—they all play as amateurs; the big money meets are a thing of the past. Jay talked to me about a series of exhibitions we could give to help him get in shape, but his heart wasn't in it.

"There is no money," he said. "Why should I go to all the trouble? For fun? Have you ever seen me play a game for fun?"

"I'm still waiting," I said.

He pulled out of the deal when the promoters wouldn't come up with plane fare for his wife.

Here we are in 1970. Bozeman is sixty-three years old and still in Vallejo. He plays golf and gin rummy, but no better than thousands of other people. There is no doubt in my mind that he could pick up a cue again and within a month be the best player in the United States. But in a world tournament? There is a good chance that it would end up with Ceulemans first, Bozeman second.

Like he says, why should he go to the trouble?

Mr. and Mrs. Joe Procita

If Joe Procita could have locked up his wife during tournaments he would have been right at the top. He could do everything with the cueball, nothing with his wife.

I was running a room one time in Los Angeles when I decided to leave town. Having a job was beginning to get to me; maybe in San Francisco I wouldn't be able to find one. The owner of the joint said to me, "McGoorty, you can't leave until you find me somebody who knows billiards, and who has a name that will draw some customers."

"I will talk to Joe Procita," I said.

"Nothing doing. He is a horseplayer."

"Listen, I am a horseplayer."

"Yes, but you are not a horseplayer like he is a horseplayer."

I argued and argued, and finally got him to say, "Okay, I will try Joe Procita, but on one condition. That you keep his wife out of here."

"How am I going to do that? I'm leaving."

"Well, get them both to promise."

I took Joe and his old lady into the bar of the Alexandria Hotel and bought them both a sarsaparilla. "Now listen," I said, "you are both pleading starvation. Here is a job for Joe that pays decent money." I knew she wanted Joe to get the job so that she would know where he was at all times.

"It would be wonderful if you could get this job for Joe," she said.

"I can get it for him, but it's up to you to keep it for him. You can be a bit of a problem at times, you know. You have got to promise to stay out of the joint."

"I promise to stay out of the joint."

Jack Kent was the owner. Nice guy, Jack Kent—paid me an extra month just to hang around and see that things went okay. All he knew about billiards was how to spell it, but he had nineteen tables and didn't want his business to disappear.

One day Joe was playing one-pocket with a guy on the front pool table. This was at noon, when Joe was supposed to be behind the counter or greeting people as they came in. When I work a room I stand by the door saying, "Hello! How are you today? Let me see if I can find you a partner . . ." You've got to be nice to people when you are in business, even people you hope will cough up a lung. Room owners today don't even try to make their paying customers feel welcome. They look at them as if they wished they would go away somewhere and shovel shit against the tide.

Joe was getting beat bad in the game of one-pocket. The other guy needed only one ball, and Joe needed a doctor. That's when his old lady came busting through the swinging doors. I guess she had come by to make sure Joe was on duty and got upset when she saw him at the table instead of behind the counter. The guy Joe was playing was just about ready to win a five-dollar bill, so to him what happened next must have looked rehearsed.

Joe's old lady walked over to the table and with both hands scrambled the balls! Swept them all down to one end! "What the hell is going on here?" she said.

The other guy dropped his cue on the floor, he was so dumfounded. His mouth dropped open and he turned his palms up. "What is this?" he said. "What is happening to me? What am I getting?"

Joe said, "Well, I, er, um, uh, er, hm, I, er . . ." That was the trouble with him—he would never speak up or put his foot down where his old lady was concerned. He would dummy up while all hell was breaking loose. Now I talk too much, I overdo it, but I admit it. At least I don't let people make me eat out of their fucking hands.

Finally Joe said, "I guess we'll have to play this game over."

"What?" the guy said. "Play it over? When I need one and you need seven? We will shit play it over."

We had a very good noontime business. We had to make our money at noon or we were dead. It looked like the guy was ready to take a poke at Joe's nose, so I stepped in and said we couldn't tolerate that sort of stuff.

"Will you pay me my five bucks, then?" the guy said to me.

I told him I had no intention of doing any such thing, but I got Joe to agree that he should forfeit the game. But he didn't have any money! He was broke! He promised to pay up as soon as his relief check came in.

Joe Procita has been on relief since 1912, which is longer than any other human being. I think he and his old lady worked it so that one of them was always collecting something. I can just hear her at the window: "My husband can't work, you know. He has that terrible cough."

On the other hand, Joe was a gentleman. A nice guy. I

played him many times in exhibitions and tournaments, and he could have taken a lot of points he didn't make. He could have screwed me many times. No, it was his old lady that was the trouble with Joe Procita. With a different old lady he would have been a different Joe Procita, which is true of a lot of people.

It is only fair to say that when they got married, his old lady didn't realize how much Joe hated work. I mean, he *hated* work. She thought he was just waiting for the right position. She had no idea of the size of the problem, didn't realize that he wouldn't take a job under *any* fucking conditions. She idolized him, and when he came home after a day in a pool hall she thought he had been applying for jobs.

The climax came at the 1952 World Tournament in San Francisco. Joe was getting beat by Masako Katsura, and his old lady was in the stands making remarks and accusing him of throwing the game. As soon as the game was over she jumped to her feet and hollered, "You let her win so you could cozy up to her!" Then she fought her way through the people, trying to get to him, waving her umbrella. He was in a crowd, moving out the door of the tournament room. She thought she saw him turn left and go into the men's can, but he didn't . . . he went straight ahead.

In the can was an old guy standing at the urinal with his Thuringer in his hand. All of a sudden Joe's old lady was beating at his head with her umbrella. The old guy hadn't even been in to see the game, didn't even know there was a tournament going on.

"You dirty bastard," she said, and let him have a good one. She didn't stop until he turned around and she saw that it wasn't Joe. It was some other guy entirely.

Good old Joe and his old lady. We had many good times together. He stuck with his wife through thick and thin, never said a word against her. I act like they're gone, but they'll outlive me by far. Last I heard they were living someplace in Chicago. I'll probably never see them again.

Masako Katsura

Masako Katsura was the greatest thing that ever happened in the whole history of billiards . . . maybe the greatest thing that ever happened, period. For a woman to compete on absolutely equal terms with men . . . and a cute, feminine woman, at that . . . why, it's never been done before or since. She wasn't competing against just any men, understand, she was competing against the greatest players in the world. She was a sensation. People who never heard of billiards before stood in line around the block for tickets to see her perform.

She showed up in San Francisco in 1949 married to a very drab potato named Greenleaf—no relation to Ralph in any way, shape, or form. This guy Greenleaf met her in Japan when he was there as a sergeant in the Quartermaster Corps. We had heard rumors about a Japanese broad who shot a good stick, but, naturally, everybody thought she probably played well *for a woman.*

When she got here she played a few exhibitions, but mainly just with local room champs, and mainly just for funsies. Oh, God, what a waste! That husband of hers didn't see the possibilities. I pee my pants thinking of the money she could have made married to somebody else. What a drawing card she was! But you couldn't talk to her about it yet because she didn't speak English, and there was no use talking to him. He was hopeless. All you could get out of him was, "Yes. No. Oh? Him. Well. Huh? Oh. Yes? No." He was dull. I kept wishing he would start chewing tobacco or something to give him some personality.

But Cochran could see the possibilities. He came out of retirement to go around playing exhibitions with her. They dressed her up in Japanese gowns, which was the smartest thing anybody ever did for her. It was Tex Zimmerman's wife's idea. She whipped up those gowns practically overnight . . . a tight fit and a slit, that's all. Tex Zimmerman's wife could do any goddam thing with a needle.

Masako was cute! She was thirty-nine years old but she looked twenty-nine. She hopped around that table on her high heels, giving the fans a little smile, and everybody loved her. Of course, her husband had to go with her on that tour. All he did was spend money. If Cochran had pheasant under glass, then Greenleaf had to have pheasant under glass. I have heard Cochran say that when he was on the road he spent fifty dollars a day. This was at a time when I was living on a nickel for coffee and sinkers.

When they got back from the tour, Cochran said to me, "McGoorty, you will have trouble with her."

"There is no question about that," I said. "I even have trouble with *you*."

At first they didn't ask me to play her. Cochran was against it. He was afraid I would break her down with my safety play and my crabbing and my general line of bullshit. And Greenleaf was against it because I wasn't his type. He was stiff, strait-laced. Puritancial is a good word. "That McGoorty," he would say, "you never know when he will come out with something vulgar." I can't feature a guy like that in the army. With General Patton! They must have had him in the back of a warehouse somewhere stacking up boxes of Kotex. I hear all kinds of stories.

Finally I got my chance at her. A game in the afternoon and a game in the evening, five days running. Did the people crowd in! They could have sold seats in the toilet.

Cochran was right—I had trouble with her. I played hard and threw her all the dirtiest stuff I knew, and I was lucky to win five out of the ten games. If you had the slightest idea of easing up on her because she was only a cute little girl, you were dead. She would murder you. I found out damned quick that you couldn't leave her an open shot. If you did she would take those balls away from you and stick them right up your pooper. The killer instinct—that broad had it, and never mind the little smile.

What a student she was, and how quick she learned! She wrote everything down in a notebook. Somebody must have told her that although I was a mean old bastard I knew a few things about billiards, because every time I took a shot she had that goddam notebook out and flipped open and her pencil busy. Sometimes I hadn't even pulled the trigger yet . . . I was still aiming . . . and I could hear the "scratch, scratch" on the sidelines. She was learning English bit by bit, too. I can remember her writing things down while I was talking to her. I always wondered if she wrote down "shit" and "fuck" and then asked Greenleaf what they meant.

I want to say right here that she was a *lady*. At all times. All the way. A perfect lady. But a killer.

She was tough to play because of the way the audience reacted to her. Every time she shot, the whole crowd leaned, hoping she would score the point. When I shot, they leaned the other way, hoping I would miss and sell the farm. I made up my mind not to do her any favors once we were in the squared circle. You had to keep control of the balls, had to keep her from breaking loose. Her short angle shots were terrific. On short angles she had everybody out looking for work.

But the best part of her game was her left-handed shooting. She flipped that cue from hand to hand like a knife and fork. All the Japanese players learn how to do it because they are so short. Left-handed she was smooth, with no awkwardness at all. Hoppe, hell, I've seen Hoppe shoot left-handed and look as clumsy as a cub bear playing with his prick.

Kilgore used to say to me, "What is she doing to you, anyway? Is she that good? I see you standing there scratching your head, wondering what move you should make. What's the big deal?"

"Listen," I said, "You'll find out. She makes you play."

Later I enjoyed it very much when she gave him a couple of good dumpings.

She was not an outstanding banker or system player, but she had a solid knowledge of the table from balkline and from years of heavy practice. She grew up in her father's billiard room, and I heard that when she was little she had to stand in the corner if she missed an easy shot. In San Francisco she practiced from eight in the morning to four in the afternoon, with one short break for a cup of tea.

It was because of her that they put on the 1952 World's Tournament in San Francisco. Christ, she drew five hundred paid customers a night all by herself. When she played they could have sold hanging room on the chandelier. She stood up well in her first big show, winning four games. The next year, in Chicago, she finished sixth in a field of eleven. She played in one more tournament, in 1954 in Argentina, and took fourth . . . fourth against the best in the world.

After that, she dropped out of competition. Some say her husband forced her to quit because he wouldn't let her go on tour without him, wouldn't let her go into rooms he didn't approve of. Then I've heard that she wanted to quit because the competition was tearing up her nerves, giving her rashes, and ruining her sleep. I think he wanted her to quit because he was jealous of her. He didn't like the attention she got.

At any rate, he's gone now and she's still here, with a lot of good years ahead of her. She has hardly touched a cue in ten years, but with her talent she could be a whiz again in no time.

Somebody should do something.

Ray Kilgore

The best piece of advice Tennessee Milliken ever gave me was when he told me not to go see Ray Kilgore dying in a hospital. "If you go," he said, "you'll regret it the rest of your life. Don't do it." But Ray was one of my best friends . . . I had to see him.

I knew Ray was awful sick, but for some reason I couldn't believe he was going to die. My God, he was only forty-five years old, the picture of health. In the hospital room there were two beds. I looked at the guy in the first bed real close; it wasn't Ray. I looked in the other bed; the guy there wasn't Ray, either.

"Well, for Christ sake," I said, "he's not in this room. Am I in the right hospital?"

When I turned to go I heard a faint voice. "Dan . . . ny. Dan . . . ny." Like a voice being blown away by the wind. I went back and looked in the first bed again. "It's me, Danny, it's me." It was Ray. He couldn't have weighed more than seventy-five pounds. A man who carried a hundred and seventy-five, shrunk down to the size of a pygmy. It was all I could do to keep from crying while I talked to him.

"Tell the boys to set up the balls for me," he said. "I'll be down to knock 'em around pretty soon. Tell 'em I'll be there pretty soon, Danny."

"I'll tell 'em, Ray."

Ray Kilgore started out as a snooker player. I met him in 1932 at Sixth and Hill in Los Angeles. He was called "St. Paul." Not only was he staying at the St. Paul Hotel, he was *from* St. Paul. He was called St. Paul for twenty years.

He had no use for three-cushion at all. Strictly snooker, and he was so good at the game that between him and Highpockets nobody had much chance around Los Angeles.

In 1941 he went off to war. By that I don't mean he went overseas—I don't think he got farther than Anaheim, where he was put to work loading trucks. The army made him a corporal because he could read a bill of lading.

In 1944 the Yakima Kid got him interested in three-cushion, and he came on fast. Fitzpatrick spotted him fifteen points on fifty at first, cut it to ten a year later, then to five. By 1952 he was so much improved that he finished fourth in the World. When he won the world championship the next year he was so happy he almost got arrested for pouring a bottle of champagne over a policeman's head.

"You played a terrific tournament, St. Paul," I said to him when he got back.

"No more of that 'St. Paul' stuff," he said. "From now on I am Raymond G. Kilgore."

How I miss the guy.

Harold Worst

Harold Worst—I can see that tall, good-looking young bastard now. I sure had no use for him at the beginning. It was at the 1950 National at Navy Pier in Chicago. He was only twenty-one years old, and called himself the World's Junior Champion, or some damned thing. I was older than his father. I had finished my five minutes of practice, which each player was allowed before the match started. As I walked back to the player's chair I waved to him that I was finished and he could take his warm-up shots. Instead, he turned to the referee. "Let's start the game," he said, "I don't need any practice to beat McGoorty."

And he didn't! I was beat the minute he said that. Of course, I was beat in any case, because he was a terrific player. I hated him for the rest of the day and part of the next. He was so cocky it made me sick, but he was a tremendous talent, and little by little as I got to know him I began to like him.

After the tournament—he didn't win it, not yet—he wanted to go back to the coast with me to look around. He got on the phone and lined up fifteen exhibition matches for us to play—Denver, Cheyenne, Salt Lake, all over. He already had leaflets printed about himself, and he sent those on ahead.

On that trip I managed to win four games out of the fifteen. I did everything I could to stop him from scoring, but it was impossible. I can remember sitting in my chair watching him shoot, marveling at what the young prick was doing to me. It was as if he had a ring in my nose and was leading me around, saying, "Now, old man, you are going to shoot from over here, and next time you are going to shoot from over there." I had to admire him.

He didn't understand why he should ever miss. After beating me about 50–32, he would call me aside and say, "You've been around a long time and know a lot about billiards. What the fuck am I doing wrong?"

He went into the service for a couple of years then, but got back in time for the 1953 tournament. He finished third, just behind Kilgore and Bozeman. The minute the thing was over he said to Kilgore, the new champion of the world, "My backers have authorized me to play you a game for any amount of money you care to put up." It was no joke; he had the backers and he had the confidence. But Ray didn't have time for that kind of thing right then—he had to pour champagne on a cop and go to St. Paul to tell his uncle about his big victory.

The next year the world tournament was in Buenos Aires. Kilgore, Cochran, Katsura, and Worst went down for it. Kilgore demanded $2,000 to risk his title, and he made them deposit it in advance in a San Francisco bank. He didn't want to go all the way to Argentina and find out that the prize would be paid in bananas.

But Kilgore didn't win. Worst won and became the youngest world champion since Hoppe. Unfortunately for him and for all of us, that was the last big professional tournament.

With billiards dying out, Harold turned to pool, and in 1965 he became world champion in that, too. Only De Oro, Johnny Layton, and Harold Worst have been tops in both games.

I saw him for the last time at a pool tournament in Las Vegas in 1966. He had lost a lot of weight and looked terrible. Like a dummy I said, "Harold! What the hell is wrong with you?"

"Danny," he said, "don't ever get cancer."

He was dead a few months later—a terrific loss to billiards.

With a few more years of competition I think he would have broken all the records.

Jim the Barber

I knew a barber who talked to billiard balls. He only did it when he thought nobody was watching. Jim the Barber was his name. Always wore a dirty hat and a felt collar. He never raised his voice, even though he got awful mad at those balls.

I was brushing tables in Graney's, a long time ago, when I saw Jim the Barber talking to the balls. When you are sweeping a floor, or emptying wastebaskets, or brushing tables, nobody pays any attention to you. They look right through you. Jim the Barber was all alone on the corner table, and he didn't notice me at all.

He had just been kissed out of a score, and he was holding a white ball in each hand. "I've told you about that a hundred times," he said to them, "and I don't want to have to tell you again." With that he rapped them together, hard, like he was spanking them. Crack, crack, crack! He put them back on the cloth and started practicing again.

I stopped brushing and watched him. When he got a kiss a few shots later, he laid his cue on the table, picked up the balls, and gave them another talking to. "You just won't learn, will you?" Crack, crack, crack!

I tiptoed over to the office, where George Helm was saying good-by to a bootlegger. We used to let the bootleggers run rampant. There were so many bootleggers coming and going they used to try to peddle grog to *each other*.

"George," I whispered, stepping inside and shutting the door, "you won't believe this, but there is a guy out there who talks to the balls like they were his kids . . . watch, you can see him from here . . ."

He didn't want to be bothered, but I got him to open the door a couple of inches. Jim the Barber was shooting the balls around as nice as could be, not saying a word.

"Change your brand of booze," George said.

"Wait, George, wait. Wait till he gets a kiss."

The guy finally took a shot with a big kiss in it. He couldn't tell which shots had kisses in them. Pow, the red ball and the cueball had a wreck before they went three feet. Down went the cue, ever so slowly. He picked a ball up in each hand. "Why do you do this to me?" he asked them. "What have I ever done to deserve it?" Crack, crack, crack! "What do I have to do to drive a simple thing through your thick skulls?" Crack! "There! Now maybe you'll behave . . ."

"Jesus Christ," George said, "now I've seen everything."

After we had a laugh in the office, George gave me a serious warning. He told me never to kid Jim the Barber about his secret. He was afraid I might get killed. I doubt that, because Jim the Barber was a harmless sort of a guy. It was only when he thought he was completely alone did he talk to the balls. I watched him do it for years. Thank God I never heard the balls answer him back.

Paul Warren

You can talk all you want about ski bums and billiard bums and people that get completely hooked on a sport, but you can't top Paul Warren. There was a real billiard nut. He played at the Rialto in San Francisco, where I worked off and on racking balls for forty cents an hour.

For a living he delivered milk cans—big ones, twenty-five and fifty gallons—to restaurants and lunch counters. One day Paul dropped a can on his big toe. He was off work for a week with his foot wrapped up, but he didn't let that interfere with his billiards; he played all day, hopping around on one leg. When he went back to his job he was still limping pretty bad. The toe kept getting worse . . . infected . . . and after about two months the croakers decided it would have to go. He had developed some kind of bone disease. Off came the toe. A year later, the foot. Then at the knee. The boys in the room took up a collection and got him an artificial leg so it wouldn't be so much work for him to play billiards. He couldn't swing milk cans anymore, so he took a job selling papers on the street corner.

Then the disease jumped to the other leg, and they started taking that one off, little by little. In a few years both legs were completely gone. But still he played billiards, every spare minute of the day! The boys in the room had put their heads together and come up with a stool with wheels. Paul sat on that and pulled himself around the table by grabbing onto the rails. He was a good player, too . . . kept improving right along, and never asked for a spot or a handicap. He wouldn't accept help on anything he could possibly do himself. Like climb the stairs to the Rialto. Near the end it took him half an hour to get up one flight of steps, but he insisted on doing it alone.

The main thing about him was that he was very good-natured. Always had a smile and a good word for everybody. He died in 1953, thirty years after he dropped that milk can on his toe.

Game-ball Shorty

Then there was Game-ball Shorty. When you are playing pool for money, a lot of money, the pressure can get pretty heavy. When you get to the game ball, the ball that wins the game, it's sometimes hard to control your nerves. Some guys clutch and dog it more than others. The worst I ever saw or heard of was Game-ball Shorty.

I knew Game-ball and I knew his old lady. He played awful good, but he had a terrible time with the winning point. It practically had to be hanging on the lip before he could knock it in.

The trouble was that when he stepped up for the final shot his eyes started rolling around in his head. He couldn't help it. Everything could have been going along real smooth. He might have the game locked up, with the last ball straight in the hole . . . but then there would go his eyes. Rolling. If I'm not mistaken they rolled in opposite directions. He would have to sit down for a minute and hold his face in his hands, go through all kinds of antics to settle himself down.

It was such agony to watch him that I never could. When he got to the last ball I always took a hike.

Big Alice

Big Alice started hanging around the pool halls of San Francisco after World War II, when she was still in high school. She was heavy even then, but nothing like she got later. Later she got so fat she had to stop and think before going through a doorway. Today she can't sit down and cross her legs—can't even begin to cross them. Well, maybe I'm exaggerating; it's just that I hate to see a nice-looking dame put on weight.

She got a lot of attention from the young studs. She was the only broad in town that hung around pool halls. She was a good player, and she was on friendly terms with everybody. When she was in a game she was the main event. Every time she bent over the table there were five thousand guys scouting the territory.

She got so good we played some exhibitions together around the San Francisco area . . . a game of three-cushion and a game of straight pool. We opened a big room in Albany and we put on a show in Berkeley when the University opened the new Student Union. I think it was in Albany that I ran a twelve off the break and followed it with a ten, but she came right back in the pool game and got a run of forty-eight.

Sometimes she talked tough, but she wasn't. She got so nervous before our exhibition at the University that she burst into tears and ran into the women's shithouse. I had to go in after her myself and coax her out.

She could have been national women's pool champ except for one thing: She wouldn't wear anything but slacks. In the women's tournaments in those days dresses were part of the deal, so she wouldn't even think of entering. Slacks trimmed her down, she thought. Why do heavy women think that? Don't they know that in slacks they look as wide as stoves? They like to wear coats, too, I suppose on the theory that it covers up their size, even if it's 110 in the shade. I've seen a million big broads in the hot sun drowning in their own sweat.

Alice eventually went all to hell, by which I mean she quit playing pool and billiards and quit hanging around. She got very religious. I've never been religious myself, though I've got nothing against it. My aunts used to say I never gave God a chance. He never gave me much of a chance, either.

Alice used to pick me up in her car and take me to Twin Peaks, where we would park and look at the scenery while she talked about Moses and some of the other guys in the Bible who couldn't run ten balls. On the way down, if I said something like, "Turn left at the next fucking corner," she would say, "At *what* corner?" And I would say, "All right, turn left at the next corner." She was trying to improve me, bless her heart.

She disappeared finally to become a nun, I heard. A nun! Come to think about it, she'll be a good one . . . provided the convent she's at doesn't have a pool table.

Part Four

•

BEYOND HUSTLING

•

1954–1970

17

The
Hate
McGoorty
Club

In 1954 for the first time in my life things were looking good for me. I had quit drinking, which nobody thought I would ever be able to do. I was only fifty-three years old, still young enough to make use of the billiard knowledge I had picked up from thirty years of playing against the world's best. The game's three superstars—Hoppe, Cochran, and Schaefer— had quit the game. Did that leave Fleet-footed Dan as the world's best player? Far from it, but it wasn't too ridiculous for me to think about winning the title. Kilgore had done it, and I had broken even in a series of exhibitions with him. There were Bozeman, Chamaco, the Navarras, and Worst—all excellent, but not completely out of reach like the big three were, especially when you consider that now I would be competing for the first time without a hangover. If I could hold my own half drunk, what would I be able to do sober? I had at least ten good years left . . . with a little luck I might be able to hit the winner's circle once or twice.

My timing was lousy. As soon as I was on the wagon, the minute I decided to pull myself together and go as high as I could in the one thing I knew, the game fell dead. Nobody realized it at the time, but three-cushion billiards died as an important sport in the United States in 1952, when Hoppe retired. It had been slipping for years; television and bowling polished it off.

As long as Hoppe was playing, promoters could make money holding professional tournaments, but the 1953 meet in Chicago, without him, drew little more than flies. Miss Katsura was good box office, but not quite good enough. Brunswick's lack of support was the final blow. The new people moving up in that company weren't billiard fans. Brunswick had built Hoppe up into a famous name, but didn't groom anybody to take his place. They quit financing the Billiard Congress of America, they quit putting billiard champions on the payroll, they quit underwriting tournaments.

Hoppe, Cochran, and Schaefer had dominated billiards for fifty years. Without them the game was finished, because the public never heard of the rest of us. Brunswick could have saved the sport. Bozeman, Worst, Kilgore, and Katsura would have kept playing if the prize money had been there, and they could have built up new followers, but it was not to be. The 1953 tournament was the last.

Which left me sucking wind. I was too old to learn how to be a legal secretary or a dental assistant. My stock took off from rock bottom and started sinking. Thank God my old lady had a decent job or we never would have made it. I would have been dead long ago without her.

I picked up a little chicken feed here and there. There was a San Francisco city tournament in 1954 at Wright's, with Catton, Harris, Rodriguez, and some other fairly good players in it, which I won, but the first prize was only a few hundred dollars. I didn't have the stomach to hit the road hustling any more—that cheap, crooked life was behind me. I started teaching billiards. There were still a few people left who were willing to pay to learn the diamond system, shot selection, safety play, position, all that stuff they would never have any use for.

Jesus, those were depressing years. Not a month went by that I didn't hear of an old, famous billiard room closing. The Chicago rooms folded up one after another until only Bensinger's was left in the Loop—out of all those great establishments I grew up in. Finally Bensinger's gave up, too, and moved to the North Side at Clark and Diversey. Sarconi's in Denver folded. Then the Rialto and Wright's in San Francisco. Finally Graney's. It was like standing on a patch of sand that the ocean was washing away.

I got awful discouraged. Billiards was dying! Nobody gave a shit! God, I could remember in the late thirties when a billiard match would draw two thousand people, and the next day only half that many would show up to watch the Chicago Bears. When the last game of a big tournament was being played, people stood in knots outside every newspaper office in the country, waiting for the flash about the outcome.

To see a game as beautiful as billiards losing out to bowling and golf, it was enough to make you turn fruit. Billiards has both offense and defense, but how can you protect yourself in bowling or golf? In bowling you are looking at the same stupid situation over and over—I think people play it so they can make a lot of noise. Golf is no better. I tried it but I couldn't see it. Maybe golf would be okay if you could leave your ball between the other guy's and the cup, to snooker him. Or if they let you use croquet rules, where you can knock his ball clear down into the fucking gulch . . . then maybe golf would be worth some attention.

I guess billiards is too tough. People won't spend the time it takes to learn it. I was teaching a guy not long ago how to pick the right shot. I set the balls up and told him that the best choice was thin off the red. Then I moved the red about an eighth of an inch to the right. "Now it is different," I said. "You shouldn't shoot the same shot because the chances of getting a kiss are a little too high. The best thing now is to turn around and shoot a force follow off the white."

He looked at the balls for a minute and then he looked at me. "You mean moving the ball just a hair changes the shot that much?"

"That's right."

"Good-by."

He hung up his cue, paid me my money, and never came in the joint again. He didn't have time to learn a game as delicate as that.

Paul Newman and Jackie Gleason gave me a little lift in 1961 when they came along with the movie *The Hustler*. A revival set in, but it was for pool, not billiards. Fancy "family style" pool-rooms started opening all over the place. I dusted off all the trick shots I knew and put quite an exhibition together. I was surprised to find out that I knew almost three hundred trick shots on a pool table. Every time one of these new joints opened I put on a show and made a hundred bucks or so, and that got me by for three or four years. I even worked in a few of them for months at a time as the resident pro. They were trying to attract a coeducational crowd, and I think they figured the housewives would go for my line of bullshit.

But the game didn't really revive much. The publicity men seemed to think that weird colors for the cloth was the secret to success. They should have asked me. I would have told them that the 1936 world's championship was played on the roof of the LaSalle Hotel in Chicago using a purple cloth and a yellow red ball. The broads didn't flock to the game then and they aren't now.

I got to be an awful sourpuss. I have always had a frown on my face, but at least when I was drinking it would go away a little and I would look almost sunny. But with no booze and the game dead I had nothing to be sunny about.

I began to notice the start of "The Hate McGoorty Club." There are no dues or anything like that. All you have to do to be a member is to pull against McGoorty, hope he loses every game, hope he gets kissed out of every point.

At the Palace Billiards in San Francisco, pretty near all the eye-fuckers are in The Hate McGoorty Club. An eye-fucker is a guy with nothing to do but watch other people. A house detective. In a poolroom he sits around keeping track of everybody. He can tell you that so-and-so is $1.36 ahead, while what's-his-name is $2.78 loser. That's an eye-fucker.

I chewed one of them out not long ago. I was playing a game for a couple of dollars, and here was this old fart sitting along the wall, eye-fucking me and getting his nuts off because I was miscuing and scratching. Finally I had all I could take.

"What's so funny, you old cocksucker?" I said. "Go somewhere and buy a piece of candy."

"Huh?" he said. "What?"

"We are playing for money, don't you know that? No, I guess you wouldn't. You wouldn't dream of putting any money behind your mouth. You wouldn't bet five cents you were alive."

Which is a big reason I am not well liked. I talk too much. I say what I think.

There are a lot of things people resent about me. If a businessman or a doctor or a lawyer takes me to dinner, everybody resents it, hates to see me get something for nothing. I haven't had to pay table time since 1934, and the other players hate me for that, too. If I have to take a leak during a pastime game I'm liable to hear, "Sure, McGoorty, take a piss, you old bastard. Take as long as you want. You don't have to pay the time." I play pastime games spotting people as many as twenty-five points on fifty, but then I try as hard as I can to win. If anybody starts talking along the sidelines I chew his ass out. If I play safe toward the end, scratching and clawing, and win the game, well, the other guy has to go to the counter to pay the time and we have another member of The Hate McGoorty Club. I can't help it—I have to play to win, even against my best friend.

Another thing is that I don't play to please the spectators. I don't go for grandstand shots. I play a lot of safety. People hate to watch defensive players. There is no doubt in my mind at all—I am serious about this—that people like to watch me play because they want to see me lose. They will pay good money at a tournament to see me get beat.

You can tell whether the audience is for you or against you by the way they lean during your shots. If I use a little body English to try to change the course of the cueball, if I start leaning, why Jesus Christ, you can bet that the audience will be leaning the *other* way. Like they had a cheerleader directing them. I watched a guy on a stool once trying to lean me out of a point . . . he fell clear off and landed on the floor with his hand in the spittoon. I notice these things . . . I see what's going on.

I am talking now about San Francisco. In other towns it's different. Even in Los Angeles. I walk into a room in Los Angeles and people actually make a fuss over me.

"Well, look who's here! Danny McGoorty! Boys, I want you to meet Danny McGoorty, the best billiard player on the coast. How the hell are you, Danny? Got any plans for dinner?"

Yes, they take me to dinner, they take me to the track, they take me around to different rooms.

But not in San Francisco:

"Look who just walked in."

"Who."

"Danny McGoorty."

"Who?"

"Danny McGoorty."

"Oh, that asshole."

You know what I mean? The sweaters and eye-fuckers lower their newspapers and say, "Oh, him. I've seen him before."

In 1962, after ten years of absolutely nothing happening except the rent, Earl Whitehead and Bob Bills decided to put on a Western States Championship in San Francisco. They thought the new interest in pool might slop over into billiards and bring enough curiosity-seekers through the turnstiles to pay the expenses. There was a ten-man field, including George Pentaris from Chicago, Joe Procita, Bill Hynes, and Homero Valdespino. By that time a lot of my old cronies had died, and the ones still around figured I was washed up, too old. I wondered if maybe they were right; I was feeling aches and pains I had never felt before. On the other hand, I knew a lot of new shots. That's one of the beauties of the game, there is always more to learn.

Naturally, I had to open the show and put up with the flash bulbs and the speeches about Ebeneezer Sneeze swallowing a cueball when he was five years old. About ten minutes before the ceremonies were supposed to start, I went into the shithouse, bought my way into a stall, and sat down on top of the lids. I wanted to be alone for a few minutes, and the shithouse was the only place. I was sitting there with my face in my hands when two old Slavonians came in and stood at the urinals.

"You gonna go in to the game todays?"

"I guess so. But that fucking McGoorty."

"Well, he knows how to plays."

"Yeah, but he's no good. He's no good."

They move over to the sinks, and I am on my tiptoes trying to see who they are.

"Well, I guess I'll buy a goddam ticket."

"Me too. And you know something? I got no use for that McGoorty, but I hope he wins."

"Me too. I don't know why."

How do you like that! Somebody had said something decent about me! I tore at the bolt on the door and came flying out of that stall. I wanted to cry and pump their hands, but they had already left. Outside the door were crowds of people going into the arena. I never did spot those two old coots or find out who they were. But they gave me a lift when I needed it.

I shot well in that meet, finishing with nine wins and no losses and averaging .899. I made my last hundred points, beating Pentaris and Procita, in eighty innings.

The next year they put on another tournament, calling it a National. Pretty much the same field, with the addition of Kubo from Japan, Fitzpatrick from Los Angeles, and Art Rubin from New York. Procita was listed, too, but he couldn't keep his wife out of the bleachers, so he had to drop out during the first game.

I wasn't so lucky this time, losing two games by a total of four points, and winding up with five wins and four losses. Rubin won with seven and two. The only thing I remember doing right was running back-to-back nines against Hynes.

Losing four games, that cheered up The Hate McGoorty Club. "He played his true game this time," the members said.

A year later some guy rushed up to me and said, "Hey, remember that tournament last year? I just figured out that if you had scored one more point against Rubin you would have beat him and you would have been in a five-way tie for first."

I love statistics like that.

"Gee," I said, "that's swell."

I should have knocked his teeth out.

18

Lunch
with
President
Kennedy

As President Kennedy once said to me . . ." I can say that and not be lying, but nobody believes me so I never say it. I met Kennedy at the White House. We had lunch together, along with about 250 other people. What he said to me was, "Nice to meet you."

"Bullshit," people say when I tell them. "You just don't go to Washington and get invited to lunch at the White House unless you know somebody. Who do you know? Nobody. Therefore, you are blowing smoke up our asses."

It's true that I don't know anybody in Washington. I don't even know J. Edgar Hoover. But I can't help it if I was picked out of a bunch of tourists along with some other people to join a big mass banquet deal. I was in town to see Washington Rags—well, yes, I do know somebody in Washington, at that, but Rags has never been elected to public office. He is a pool player, and since I was on the east coast he wanted to pick my brains for anything

I might know about the speed of certain players he hadn't seen in a while. How many points could Three-Fingers Whitey give Peoria Paul, that sort of thing.

With some time to kill, I drifted over to the White House to take a look around. There was a tour of some kind moving through the gates, so I tagged along. Inside we walked back and forth in various hallways while a guy told us the history of the joint. It isn't like a home at all; it's more like a museum. Apparently there is a long story to tell about every doorknob and wastebasket. "The ashtray we are passing on your left was a gift from the Queen of Mexico."

I was watching for the Men's Room when two guys arguing pretty heavy came out of a side door. "That is a very big table," the one was saying, "and you can't fill it at a minute's notice." "You had all week." "Nobody told me." Back and forth like that. Here was the deal: There was some kind of luncheon on tap for foreign food merchants and they hadn't invited enough people to fill up the table. It was half an hour before noon and so they were rounding up a few gawkers to fill the empty chairs. A guard told me that they sometimes plan in advance to grab a few tourists at the last minute and run them into one of these big banquets to give them a thrill of a lifetime.

The two guys that were arguing gave our bunch the once-over and then waved to me and about six others who were well dressed and looked harmless to follow them. Like always, I was dressed to the teeth.

Whenever I have tried to tell this story, it is along about here that people start getting up and walking away, waving their arms and saying, "Holy Christ, have you been listening to that fucking McGoorty today?" But I can't help it.

What happened next is that they took us one at a time into a little room. They don't let you within nine hundred yards of the President before they interview you, find out who you are, even frisk you, to make sure you won't ruin the party.

I sat down in front of a guy at a desk, a college-graduate type. He asked me questions and jotted things down on a form he had on a clipboard.

"What are your interests, your hobbies?"

The idea was that the President would have a list to glance at so that he could make small talk if he had to with anybody at the table. Say the woman in seat 36 trips and falls in his lap. He can look down the list to 36 and then say to her, "How are your violets doing?"

My main interests. I couldn't very well say ponies, pussy, and Panther Piss, so I said, "Billiards."

"Billiards? You mean, like, pool?" He made a sawing motion.

"Yeah, like that, but I mean billiards."

"I will put down 'pool.' "

"Listen," I said, "that is your piece of paper and you can put down whatever you want, but if you want to put down my main interest you will put down 'billiards.' "

"I'm afraid I . . ."

"Pool tables have pockets. Billiard tables don't. I am a three-cushion billiard player."

"Ohhhhhhhh. Willie Hop's game."

Years ago anybody who rhymed Hoppe with pop instead of poppy would have been thrown in jail. "That's right," I said. "Willie Hop's game."

"And what is your occupation, Mr. McGoorty?"

I wish I would have had the nerve to pull my chair up close, lower my voice, and say, "I am in town to sell some information." It was true. Rags would spring for dinner, at least. Actually, I didn't even think of saying that at the time. "Billiards," I said.

"No," he said, "your *occupation*. Billiards is your *hobby*."

"Billiards."

"Billiards is your occupation? What you do for a living?"

"That's it. You've got it."

He shook his head. He even laughed a little as he scribbled a long paragraph on the sheet. "I don't believe we've ever had a professional billiard player before," he said.

He gave me some coaching. He told me that there would be people there from all over the world with samples of their national food, and that they would come around and show it to me. When I had seen enough I was supposed to say, "Thank you very much," otherwise they would show it to me again. They had all been told that "thank you very much" was the signal to beat it.

The banquet was in a room with a table a block long. People were everywhere. There were ninety-five nations in the U.N. at that time, and I'll bet every one of them had somebody taking in this free feed. People were wearing their national costumes . . . you know, wrapped up in sheets and so forth. I strolled around nodding and smiling, trying to act as if I hoped everybody was being well treated in my country.

Kennedy came in. He was a tall sonofabitch! A fine-looking man. I think anybody would have said that he was a fine-looking man. He started in shaking hands, but I hung back, not wanting to get involved. Pretty soon I realized that he was bound and determined to shake hands with everybody in the room. He started working his way toward me, coming down the line I was in. I was more or less taken by surprise, and when he was about four people away I pissed my pants. I don't mean I splashed all over the floor, but I do mean that two or three drops leaked out.

"Nice to meet you," he said, giving me a quick squeeze. I was struck dumb, and gave him a frown and a limp fish. I thought he might ask me about the bank shot I made against the Alhambra Flash in 1937, but I guess he didn't know my number. He went right on to the next guy.

A little later a foreigner came up to me with a salesman's display case. I guess I was supposed to know where he was from by the outfit he had on, but I didn't have any idea. He opened the case and showed me rows of little pieces of dried fish, I think. I looked at it and he looked at me and I looked at him and he lifted up the tray to show me another layout of dried fish underneath.

"Looks like good stuff," I said.

He pointed to each tidbit.

"Very nice," I said. I gave him a little salute as if to say "so long," but he just stood there.

Then he said, "Five dollars."

"Five dollars?"

"Five dollars."

Was that what it sold for back home, or was that what he would unload it for here?

"Listen," I said, "you've got the wrong customer. I'm lucky if I have a dollar thirty-nine on me."

A guard came over and asked me if I was having any trouble.

"Well," I said, "I think this gentleman wants to sell me some fish, but I don't have change for a wet match."

"If you are finished looking at his samples, protocol suggests that you say, 'thank you very much.' "

"Yeah, well, thank you very much, but I've got to get out of here. I've got another appointment."

I got out as fast as I could. I didn't even say good-by to the President or ask him and the Mrs. to drop by my room at the Gotham.

19

Ceulemans
and the
New
Amateurs

Damned if three-cushion billiards didn't start showing a little life in 1966 . . . about fifteen years too late as far as I was concerned. It never did die in Japan, South America, and Europe, where all kinds of tournaments are held, but on an amateur basis. The players get their travel and living expenses paid, but don't play for prize money. It is a hee-haw proposition, like the Olympics.

In 1966 some billiard nuts organized the Billiard Federation of the U.S.A. and put on a world invitational amateur tournament in San Francisco. They asked me to play because they wanted at least one old man in it. I would have to play the six best foreign players they could find, the champion and runner-up from Japan, South America, and Europe. There was one guy in particular that everybody wanted to see: Raymond Ceulemans of Belgium, only twenty-nine years old and already World Champion five times. His tournament averages were unbelievable: one point three, one point four, one point five. Higher than anything Hoppe or Cochran ever made. But I knew that amateur rules were easier than the rules I was used to. I wondered what Mr. Ceulemans would do when he ran into a little old-fashioned American safety.

I found out. He scored.

Before the tournament started I thought it would never come off. I was so convinced that billiards in the United States was dead and buried that I thought the foreign players wouldn't show up, or maybe the fifteen guys who were putting up the financial guarantee would get cold feet. But nothing went wrong. The players arrived from all parts of the world, a beautiful arena was set up at the San Francisco Elks Club, I was interviewed by the Chronicle and the Examiner, and it was like old times.

Ceulemans turned out to be a cheerful character, built like a tree trunk, about five foot ten and weighing about 190. Solid. Powerful looking, with something hard in his eyes that I didn't notice in the other players. When he first showed up I was talking to a friend of mine about pussy, saying that at my age the only way you could keep a girl friend was make sure you didn't break any fingers. An interpreter put that into French and Ceulemans laughed, but for all I know the interpreter told him something else entirely.

I was in the front-row seats for his first game, anxious to see if he deserved to be ranked with the all-time greats. His bridge was funny looking, and he used a cue with a tiny tip only about eleven millimeters across. He was not flashy. He took his time. I saw that he was solid at the table and knew exactly what he wanted to do at all times. I saw perfect control of speed and saw management of all three balls. But his choice of shots and his general style of play is so different from Cochran and Hoppe it is hard to compare them.

During my game with him I sat in my chair and watched him do things that to me are cardinal sins. Like dying on the white ball. When you die on the white ball you stand a good chance of selling out if you miss. But he didn't miss. He always made the point. The cueball might go thirty feet and just barely reach the white, but it would reach. Or he would shoot a shot that figured to leave all three balls in the center part of the table, a dangerous shot defensively. Gradually it began to sink in that Mr. Ceulemans pays more attention to position than safety; he concentrates on what he is going to do instead of worrying too much about what you might do. When you are as accurate as he is you can afford to think like that.

He uses a short bridge and gets action on the cueball that doesn't make sense. After seeing how the cueball acted on one of his shots I had a notion to grab it and chop it in half with a hatchet to see what was inside.

I said he was not flashy, but he is a good showman, in his way. He can't be hurried. He doesn't buckle under pressure. He sometimes takes what I think is the wrong shot, but then he is only a baby.

The man is a hell of a player, there is no doubt about it. If you leave him any kind of opening at all, he will score. He simply does not miss. It is hard to say just how good he is because he dominates every tournament. When I saw him in Las Vegas in 1970, I told him that if he kept improving he would kill the game all over the world, which he took as a joke.*

Ceulemans is not the only one of the foreigners who has got to be put in the top rank. There is also Ogata, from Japan. He is a very solid player, and he would be even better if he oiled his shoes. You can't walk around a billiard table for a couple of hours with squeaky shoes and not have it start eating into your brain.

I played fairly well in that 1966 tournament, averaging .833, but I still wound up with a double handful of shit. My rented tux

---

*Ceulemans went on to win twenty-nine world championships and is still a force in the year 2003 at the age of 66. —RB

didn't fit right and I won only two games, one of them over a former world champion, Suarez of Peru. Me and the two other American entries, Hynes and Kashiki, finished last, a pretty sad picture for a country that used to lead the world.

It was a strange tournament for me. I was used to playing in an atmosphere of blood and hate and money. The sportsmanship and politeness of those foreign characters bothered me quite a bit, kept me off balance. They actually seemed happy for you when you did something right! And the Japanese players, holy Christ, when they got kissed into a point by accident they apologized! They turned to you and gave you a little bow, right when you felt like wrapping your cue around their fucking necks.

Take the final game. Ceulemans and Navarra tied for first and had to play a decider. This was Enrique Navarra, the uncle of Juan and Zeke. When Ceulemans got off a run of sixteen, Navarra got out of his chair and gave him a hug! Jesus Christ! And when Navarra made the game point, which put Ceulemans out of the winner's circle for the first time in years and years, Ceulemans threw his arms around him, patted him on the back, and told him how happy he was for him, instead of giving him a knee in the balls the way any American professional would have. I've never seen anything like it.

That tournament was my one and only performance as an amateur. Play for the fun of it? Not me. As far as I am concerned, the idea of a tournament is to try to win the prize money. The pressure of competition, the effort of trying to play your best, the strain of playing in front of an audience that is hoping you'll rip your fly open on the corner of the table . . . I don't see anything fun about it. You should get paid to do it.

Kubo and Ogata invited me to come over to Japan to play some exhibition matches. They said they liked my style because I played all the old-time shots. My expenses would be paid, but that's all, so I turned them down. Will a plumber unclog your toilet for the fun of it?

My friends thought I was crazy. Turn down a free trip to Japan? "The girls," they told me. "You should go to Japan for the girls."

"Why should I go anywhere because of the girls?" I asked them. "It takes me a week now to screw my wife."

In 1968 Juan Navarra came to town, calling himself the professional champion of South America, which wasn't far wrong, I suppose. He had just come from Mexico City, where he beat Chamaco 300–275. Bob Bills, who owns the Palace Billiards in San Francisco, set up a 75-point match in his joint.

This guy Juan Navarra has a powerful stroke and always puts on a good show for the spectators. He has a trick shot exhibition that is out of this world. One trick shot that he and his brother Zeke practice back home in Argentina can't be made unless the table is on the second floor. They put two object balls side by side in the gutter outside on the street. Then they go back upstairs and shoot the cueball off the table so that it bounces through the door and down the steps. If the cueball hits those two balls in the street, which it does about once every two years, they go around smiling for a week.

Juan told me before we started the game that he was organizing an invitational professional tournament in Venezuela to pick a new world professional champion, and one reason for his tour was to check out some of the American players. That should have told me something, but it didn't. I was dumb enough to beat him 75–51 in seventy-five innings. If I had any brains I would have let him win and got invited to the Big Show. Instead, he invited Pentaris of Chicago, a guy he knew he could beat. I heard later that Juan won that tournament and now calls himself World Champion. That could have been me.

Old-timers who saw me beat Navarra that night in 1968 said I never played better. I was sixty-seven years old, but my eyesight was still sharp and my control of speed was still good. I had a few new aches and pains, but I figured I could last for quite a few more years at near my peak. Maybe I would still get a chance to win something big. Maybe I would be Alfredo De Oro all over again—I was mean enough and crusty enough.

Then I noticed blood in my spit.

20

In the
Arms
of the
Croakers

I have never been what you would call healthy, but I could never afford complaints. Varicose veins in my legs have bothered me for thirty years, but what was I supposed to do about them? I went to a croaker once to have them looked at and he started sharpening a knife. "It will cost you $375 for this one and $450 for that one," he said, pointing at my legs.

"Good-by," I said.

Most of my life I have had a hangover. I felt very out of sorts when I didn't. My solution for everything, including medical problems, was to have another drink. When I quit drinking my varicose veins didn't go away, the cyst on my back didn't go away, and neither did the piles in my pooper, which at times are like a bunch of grapes. In fact, since I have been sober I seem to feel my aches and pains more. In the last ten years my frown has got so deep it is a chore to smile. I don't enjoy smiling.

Feeling rotten, though, has never seemed to bother my game. I have heard that when I start bitching and moaning during a tournament, money starts going down on me, people start betting on me.

A man who used to own seven meat markets in Chicago came to see me one day in late 1969, a man I have known for forty years. He knocked at my door and came in and sat on the edge of my bed. My wife had left town to get a better job, so I was living alone.

"Let's go on a trip," my friend said. "Anywhere you want. I'll pay all the bills. Fiji. Bermuda. Anywhere. What do I care what it costs? I'm all through. Been spitting blood. All day long. Look . . ."

We went into the can. He hacked up an oyster and spit it into the toilet. I saw fresh blood. Red. Bright.

"Jesus," I said, "you've got to see a doctor right away."

"I've already seen a doctor. I've seen a dozen doctors. They cut me open, took a look, and sewed me back up. I'm all through, Dan. Cancer. You go around town and pick up some travel leaflets. Let's go somewhere where the girls don't wear any clothes. Call me in a few days when you decide. It makes no difference to me, so please yourself."

I felt awful bad about it, because he was one of my oldest friends. But I never picked up any travel leaflets, and we never went on any trip. Three days after he paid me that visit I hacked an oyster into the sink and saw some blood of my own. Now it was my turn.

A doctor pounded on my chest with his fingers.

"Does this hurt?"

"No."

"Does this hurt?"

"No."

"You're sure this doesn't hurt?"

"Yes."

"This hurts, doesn't it?"

"No." He was getting mad because nothing he did hurt. He gave up on the pounding.

"How do you feel?"

"Fine. But I am burning up."

"That is because you may have pneumonia. I am putting you in the hospital."

I didn't even have a chance to go back to my room to pick anything up. Right into the hospital I went. The intensive care ward, where they keep the rails up on the bed and where somebody sits near you at all times reading a Diamond Dick novel. They gave me sleeping pills, then woke me up to stick a needle in my arm, poke a finger up my ass, or ask me to bleed, spit, or piss. Spit samples five times a day, and almost as many blood tests. Every goddam medical student who walked down the hall came into my room and stuck his finger up my ass.

My temperature bounced around between 100 and 104. They were sure I had pneumonia, but they got tired of testing my spit and pounding on my chest saying, "You mean to tell us this doesn't hurt?"

I was not their favorite patient. I didn't cooperate and I didn't give the answers they wanted. I squawked about my room, which had four other dingbats in it, most of them delirious. The doctor in charge of me got furious. "Why did your temperature go up today?" he said.

"How the hell should I know? Why don't you ask a doctor?"

I didn't pull any punches with those birds. Being polite gets you absolutely nowhere. And I was scared. I could see the blood in my spit. If I was dying I sure as hell wasn't going to be polite about it. And I had a hunch that I was dying. So did the doctors, but they couldn't prove it, which was why they were mad.

"I'll give you something to make your temperature go down. You can go home if you keep it down."

"If I keep it down? Now just how the fuck do you suppose I am going to be able to do that?"

"By keeping calm. How is your urine stream?"

"Did you ask me how my urine stream was?"

"Yes. Is it strong or weak?"

"For the love of Christ. It's strong enough to put out a fire in a wastebasket."

"You always make a joke out of everything, don't you, Mr. McGoorty?"

"I'm not laughing; this is no joke to me. I've been poked, stabbed, and cornholed by every sonofabitch in this hospital. The whole staff has had a finger up my ass, and still nobody knows anything."

"You may have gallstones."

"Yes, I may. I certainly may. I may have anything in the fucking book. But what do I have?"

"We may have to operate."

"Will that make my temperature go down?"

"No."

"Well, let's operate, then."

"We better have an x-ray."

"I've had an x-ray. I've had thirty-seven x-rays."

"We better have another x-ray."

What a hospital. First I waited in line to take a piss, then I waited in line to have an x-ray. They put me on a table and wheeled me down to the basement at some odd hour of the night and parked me in a cold, marble hallway where the wind came through at ninety miles an hour. The x-ray man showed up eventually and gave me a look as much as to say, "You dirty son-ofabitch, why couldn't you wait till tomorrow?" A real nice guy.

My spit cleared up and my temperature went down so they

let me go home. Then my temperature went up. Back into the hospital. In and out, in and out, month after month. They couldn't figure out what was ailing me. Everybody in the hospital had a theory.

A young kid came up to my bed and said, "I am Doctor Chapps."

I couldn't believe it. "You? A doctor?"

"Yes. I am a resident doctor."

"You mean you're an intern?"

"Well, here we call them resident doctors."

"Look, kid, what do you want?"

Turned out that he was interested in a red spot the size of a pinpoint that I've had on my finger since 1910. He wanted to probe it. Take a sample of it and study it. Write a big article about it. I told him nothing doing. "Take a hike," I said.

The blood tests! Oh, how they love to get that blood out of you! They don't want to pay twenty-five bucks for it from volunteers when they can get it free from patients. Free? What am I saying! They charge you fourteen bucks to take it out of you. I got so tired of people coming in my room with a fistful of test tubes they wanted filled that I put a stop to it.

"Who ordered this blood test?" I said.

"Why, doctor so-and-so."

"He's not my doctor. Get lost."

"Oh, but he's an associate of your doctor."

"But he's not my doctor. I've had five blood tests already today. Nobody gets another drop from me unless I see a written order from my doctor with the reason for it in words I can understand."

A few minutes later another, older man came in to try to talk some sense into me.

"Mr. McGoorty. Don't you realize that your body is making blood all the time? Even while we talk, while you lie there, it is making blood."

I blew up at that. "And what the hell do you think it is making blood for? So I can throw it away? So you guys can take it downstairs and stare at it and see imaginary germs in it and write reports on it?"

I put a stop to the cornholing, too. No more fingers up my pooper without written orders. What they do is use you as guinea pig and a lump of clay for the medical students. "Go up to room 453 and stick your finger in McGoorty's ass. Maybe you will learn something." My God, one giant came in my room and without so much as a how-do-you-do started putting on a rubber glove the size of a catcher's mitt. He would have torn me apart if I hadn't been awake and strong enough to do some shouting.

But, you know, I was treated pretty well in general. The meaner I got, the better I was treated. The nurses especially seemed to take a liking to me, and I didn't slip them money to have their hair done, either. I didn't give them a thing, except a lot of bullshit. They got enough bullshit from me to last a lifetime.

In March they let me out of the hospital for a few weeks and told me to eat well and take it easy because they wanted me as strong as possible for a bronchoscopy. I didn't know what a bronchoscopy was then, but I know what a bronchoscopy is now. It is the most horrible thing ever put on the face of this earth. They put me on my back on a table with my head hanging over the edge. One guy held my mouth open by grabbing my lower teeth, while two other assholes came at me with lights and instruments. They used a suction pipe like dentists do, but they stuck it down my gullet. All of this was with a local, not a general, so I knew just what they were doing. Finally, when they had me just the way they wanted me, they made me swallow the sword.

They were trying to look around inside my lungs, but they didn't see anything interesting, which made them mad. They couldn't get down far enough, they told me later, as if it was partly my fault.

Somebody had the idea of slitting my throat, so they did. Nothing. They found nothing. They were sure I had cancer by now, I know that, but they never used the word. You should have seen the forlorn, ugly-tempered people I was dealing with . . . people who knew I had cancer but couldn't prove it. Day after day they hunted for it.

Then they found it. In my chest, with a biopsy. They came at me with a big needle with a smaller needle inside of it, and they plunged that cocksucker into my chest and came up with a sample of my insides. What they had was a piece of malignant tissue. Oh, were they happy! "We found it! We found it!" They had found cancer so close to my heart that they couldn't operate, and you should have seen the smiles. I was a tough nut to crack, but they worked hard and did their best and finally were able to prove that I was a hopeless case. "We found it! It was in his chest!" Jesus Christ, everybody on the floor knew it in no time. I had twenty mourners in the room the next day—nurses, residents, patients, everybody.

All the attention I got, it pissed me off. There have been plenty of times in my life when I could have used some attention and some medical help, but nobody would give me any. No, they waited until it was too late. The way they worked on me and consulted about me when they couldn't find that cancer! I bothered them; I was an interesting puzzle. After sixty-nine years of paying no attention to me they brought in the best brains in medicine and all the latest scientific gear in order to prove one thing: that I was a terminal cancer patient and that nothing could be done for me. I had a wonderful case of terminal cancer, a swell case, so all the medical students came by again to have a gander at me.

One doctor said I had six months to live, another guessed

eight months, another said twelve to eighteen months. They couldn't even agree on when I was supposed to die.

Since Medicare came along just in time to pay my bills, they decided to give me a series of cobalt treatments. I lived in my room at the Gotham and went to the hospital two or three times a week for a couple of months. They put a gown on me and put me on a table and lowered a big machine over me that looked like something out of a science-fiction movie. Two nurses marked points on my chest and measured the distance between the machine and the points. Then everybody left the room. One guy kept an eye on me by looking through a porthole behind a thick pane of glass. The first time they switched on the machine it felt like my ears were all of a sudden stopped up, there was no air, I had no feeling. I was tied down, so all I could do was lie there and listen to the Rrrrrr, Rrrrrr, and look at the spot on the machine that the rays came out of, although they are invisible. I felt myself getting warm, especially my chest, so I knew something was going into me. I couldn't see it, but I could feel it.

When they wheeled me out of there I said to the nurse, "It got pretty warm, there, until you switched it off. I was getting a little worried."

"What was getting warm?"

"The cobalt rays, I guess. I could feel my chest getting warm."

"You didn't feel anything. There is no heat from it."

All that stuff I thought I was feeling, it was just my imagination.

At first they had me under that gun five times a week, first on my back, then on my stomach. It practically knocked me out—I couldn't see straight and I couldn't even get up off the litter. They called some big shots over to look at me, put me in a private room, and studied me for two hours. I got the rubber glove again. Man, without that rubber glove cancer wouldn't be where it is today. To have some sonofabitch slip on a rubber glove, smear it with vaseline, then jam it up your ass and run it around in circles while he talks to the nurse about what he is going to do on the weekend . . . well, nothing much worse can happen to you.

The upshot was that they decided they had the juice turned up too high. They were giving me more than I could stand, and damned near killed me with the cure. But by putting me in that private room for a few days they could send some nice big bills to Medicare.

Medicare works this way. In the hospital everything is paid for except things like electrocardiograms and medicine you take home. But if you are an outpatient . . . brother, watch out, because they are going to nail you with every goddam thing imaginable. Of course, for some of it you only pay twenty percent, but that is still enough to ruin you, especially if the only thing you can hock is a twenty-ounce cue.

Once they sent me the same bill six times. I paid it the first time, but they kept sending me a new one. Each time I sent it back after writing across it: this bill is paid. Finally I took it in person right out to the hospital and asked for Mrs. Humperdink herself, or whatever her name was. When she came to the counter I laid the bill down and wrote this bill is paid on it and handed it to her.

"You are not allowed to write on the bill," she said.

"And you are not allowed to send me bills that are paid."

You have to keep a sharp eye out or those hospitals will rob you blind. You can be sound asleep and have some visiting doctor sneak in your room and stick a finger up your ass and when you scream bloody murder he will run down the corridor and mail you a bill for $57.50.

I have learned a few things about hospitals, being in and out of them so many times lately. One day I am admitted at one in the afternoon. "I'll get you something to eat," says the nurse.

"No thanks," I say, "I'm not hungry."

"Well, I better get you a little something."

"No, no, don't get me nothing to eat. I don't want nothing to eat."

"Oh, but you should have something to eat . . ."

"Listen, I don't want nothing to eat."

See what she is doing? If she can get me to eat the noon meal the hospital can charge me and the government for another half day. I'm onto all those tricks now.

Or say you are scheduled to be released from a hospital at eleven in the morning, when your doctor is supposed to give you a final check. Well, you better get dressed and walk out of the place, because that doctor is not going to show until 11:02, which means that the hospital can charge you for another half day, or at least they can stick you five dollars for an extra hour.

A lot of this stuff is covered in the fine print in the Medicare contract you sign, but they hand it to you when you are too sick to think.

They are making a fortune. One doctor practically admitted it to me. I had to see him after being in the hospital for a week. "By the way," he said, "how much was your bill this time?"

"Nine hundred and ninety-five dollars and eighty cents."

"That sounds about right. We try to keep it up to at least a hundred and thirty a day."

I took thirty-four cobalt treatments, and they did some good. They shrank my tumor down to a much smaller size, but they killed my appetite. I had to force food down my throat to stay alive. The only way I could find the strength to eat was to remember how Ray Kilgore looked at the end.

The Hate McGoorty Club could see me failing. I began to look like a mummy. I still gave a few lessons at the Palace Billiards—that was my only source of income—but I even had to quit that when I got too weak to demonstrate the shots properly.

At least a dozen people asked me if I wanted to sell my cue. They closed in on me like vultures.

To one guy I said, "You've got a lot of fucking guts to ask me to sell my cue."

"What do you mean?" he said, real surprised. "What are you going to be needing it for?"

But there were days when I felt pretty strong, days when I half-believed I was going to pull off a miracle and get better. One day I practiced three-cushion for a while and got off a run of seven and another of eight. My game seemed to be as good as ever. On my way back to the Gotham I walked past a bar in the tenderloin, and through the door I could see a kid playing pool by himself on one of those coin-operated tables. It was a neighborhood joint with old men and women from the rooming houses around there sitting on the stools. The kid was big and strong, looked something like Jerry Quarry, the boxer. Without stopping to think if I was strong enough, I asked him if he wanted to play a couple of friendly games for a dollar. He did, and before I knew it I was four games ahead. It was like old times. I hadn't hustled a game of pool in ten years, and I was so out of practice that I made a beginner's mistake: I was playing a stranger and I forgot to collect after every game.

"Listen," I said to him when I felt myself getting tired, "you owe me four dollars. I'm not playing any more until you pay me." I kept my voice low so the customers at the bar couldn't hear. They weren't paying any attention to us and I wanted to keep it that way.

The kid leaned over to me. I thought he was going to whisper something, but instead he shouted as loud as he could: "Try and get it, you old fart!"

That's what he hollered, right in my ear, with a grin on his face. He had no intention at all of paying me. Everybody in the joint was swiveled around and staring at us. There was nothing I could do, because that kid could have picked me up by the shirt-front and hung me on the wall like a suit of old clothes. I laid my cue down and walked out, with all the eyes on my back. My ears rang like a gong for an hour from that shout.

The Gotham Hotel. Not the greatest place in the world to go home to. It was going downhill faster than I was. At one time it was considered a very classy place, and some of the top pimps in town stayed there, but the town moved off in another direction, the auto dealers took over the neighborhood, and a freeway ramp moved in next door. A couple of years ago they fired the elevator operator, then the bellboys. Then they fired the desk clerk and started locking the front door. A hotel that's sinking fast. Next thing you know it'll be torn down and hauled away, and you can say the same for me.

Guess who paid me a visit today! A cemetery salesman! This is no shit. I think he got my name from the cancer clinic. I think they find out who all the terminal patients are, then pay them a little visit. He sat on my bed and spread out all his brochures, with colored pictures of all the things he had to offer. Now when I die I don't care if they just carry me out in a bucket, but that wouldn't be very nice for my wife, so I am going to go along with whatever she wants. It's her money.

This particular cemetery doesn't plant too many people in the ground any more. They put you in a mausoleum that has walls full of what look like safety deposit boxes. The top row must be fifteen feet above the ground, which is where I picked a spot. A package deal for fifteen hundred bucks, with the slot below mine reserved for my wife. I've always tried to get a room on the top floor of every hotel I've ever lived in. Having people walking around on top of me makes me nervous.

●

Danny McGoorty died of cancer on November 1, 1970,
at the age of sixty-seven.

●

Appendix

The Rules of McGoorty's Games

Three-Cushion Billiards

For the first half of his life, McGoorty made his living hustling straight pool (see rules below), rotation, and nine-ball, though nine-ball before World War II wasn't nearly as popular as it is today. What he enjoyed most and what he was best at was three-cushion billiards, an elegant and artistic game that requires a high level of imagination to play well. The great three-cushion players have a control over cueball spin, carom angles, and speed that is positively uncanny.

Three-cushion is played on a pocketless table five feet wide and ten feet long, considerably larger than a pool table. Only three balls are used, a red ball and a cueball for each player. A point is scored when a player manages to make his cueball hit three or more cushions and one ball, in any order, before hitting the other ball. In other words, the cueball must hit the other two balls to score, but before it hits the second one it must contact three or more cushions. Within those simple definitions lie a world of beauty, creativity, and nuance.

The game is won by the first player to reach a predetermined number of points. A half-dozen or so players in the world can average 1.500 points per turn at the table. A run of

Diagram A

ten points in a row is very good, twenty is terrific, thirty is the stuff of legends. See the diagrams for a few of the many ways to score.

In the lower shot in Diagram A, the player hits the left side of the red ball and sends the cueball off three rails to the other ball for a point. (For simplicity, I have drawn only the path of the cueball.) It is not necessary to hit the red ball first. At the upper left corner of the diagram, the cueball hits two rails first, the white ball, then the other white ball. Hitting the same rail twice is perfectly legal. In the upper right corner of the diagram is a "double-the-rail" shot. By using extreme right-hand sidespin, the cueball is made to hit three rails first, then the red, then the white.

In Diagram B on the next page is a very common pattern: the twice-around-the-table shot. The shot is easier than it looks to a beginner because if the cueball misses the red ball going into the corner it will almost surely hit it on the way back out, making it a six- or seven-rail shot. A good player would consider this a high-percentage shot.

For an introduction to the game, call 1-800-828-0397 and order "The Best of Three-Cushion, Volume 1" from Accu-Stats Video Productions. The tape starts with a demonstration of basic patterns followed by fifty great shots filmed live at world tournaments. You'll find 200 three-cushion diagrams in *Byrne's New Standard Book of Pool and Billiards,* Harcourt Brace & Company, 1998. Also see shots online at caromcafe.com.

Straight Pool

It's amazing how many young players—and older players who play only in taverns—don't know the game of straight pool, also known as "14.1 Rack." A few decades ago it was very popular and was the only game considered for tournaments among top players. Two of the greatest players in the history of pool, Ralph Greenleaf and Willie Mosconi, played it to the near exclusion of other pocket games. (Both men also played excellent three-cushion.) Nine-ball had nearly swept it from

Diagram B

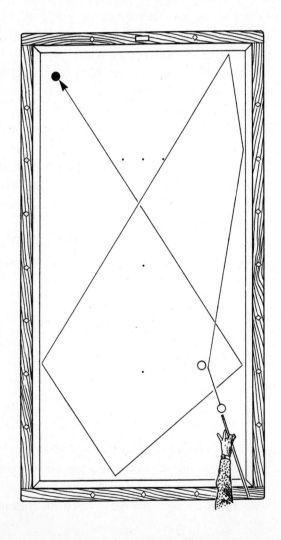

the field because it is better suited to television, thanks to its faster pace. All top nine-ball players, however, play good straight pool, and for students of the game there isn't anything better for teaching close control of the cueball. An essential skill is the ability to plan ahead and see the best way to attack an array of balls.

It is a call-shot game, meaning that the player must call a ball and a pocket. The shot counts even if the ball goes in the called pocket by a path not intended or foreseen—to that extent luck counts. The balls can be pocketed in any order and each ball counts one point. When only one ball is left on the table, the rest are racked as shown in the diagram. Players try to leave the cueball in a position from which the fifteenth ball can be made and the cueball sent into the rack to spread the balls; in that way the run can be continued. A perfect position is shown in Diagram C, next page. A hard, accurate stroke will send the object ball into the corner pocket while at the same time the cueball will break the rack apart.

Unless you are an experienced shotmaker and position player, you won't find it easy to run fourteen balls and leave yourself a good break shot. The best professionals can run hundreds of balls without a miss on today's 4 × 9 foot tables. McGoorty was justifiably proud of his high run of 74 on a five-by-ten-foot table with tight pockets, which was standard equipment when he was learning the game.

To see how the game should be played, order any one of several straight pool tapes available from Accu-Stats.

Detailed rules of straight pool, three-cushion, nine-ball, eight ball, and other games are given in *The Official Rules and Records Book* published by the Billiard Congress of America and available at billiard supply stores.

Diagram C

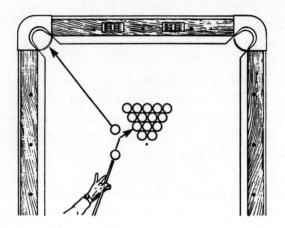

Name Index

---

*Pseudonym

*Pseudonym

The Broadway Library of Larceny

The Library of Larceny is a collection of books about—and sometimes by—people who exploit public confidence for their own personal monetary gain. Some of them are thieves pure and simple. Some are get-along types who just happen to be standing nearby with pockets flapping when spoils are divided. And some are con artists—with equal stress on the second word of that formula—men and women who do not steal, exactly, and certainly never employ violence or strong-arm tactics, but who extract sums by means of a sort of psychic jiujitsu from pigeons who are often all too willing to be plucked. These books fall into the true-crime genre, but that genre (once dominated by pipe-smoking sleuths) has lately been given over almost entirely to depressing psychopathology and gore for gore's sake. The Library of Larceny proposes instead to restore property crime to its full, glorious stature. It is, after all, a portion of the inheritance of this Land of Opportunity.

The books in the series highlight the ingenuity of their subjects, their delight in the aesthetics of their profession, their artisanal pride in a neatly turned score, and, not incidentally, their pleasure in language. For whatever reasons, swindling seems to awaken in its perpetrators a gift for vigorous, highly colored language, with accompanying deadpan humor. The metaphors so often come from the natural world—a victim is a "doe" or an "apple"; he or she is "lop-eared"; a dollar bill is a "fish" or a "bumblebee"—that it is as if we were listening to lions and tigers discussing their jobs. Add to all this an inside view of a world of poolrooms and racetracks and bars and brothels, the raffish world of professional leisure. The books will span the past century, stretching from the time after the West had been won—and the wildlife that had evolved along the way sought new outlets for its talents—right up to the present era of corporate malfeasance, by way of the hectic, wised-up city life of the cocktail age. The books, many of them long out of print, will appeal to a wide range of readers, young and old: hipsters, pirates, roués, scalawags, poets, armchair psychologists, advertising strategists, cultural theorists, promoters, touts, sibyls, and bon vivants everywhere.

Luc Sante
Series Editor

About the Author

Robert Byrne, the bestselling author in billiards history, has written seven books on the game, including *Byrne's New Standard Book of Pool and Billiards* (1978, 1998) and *Byrne's Complete Book of Pool Shots* (2003), and appears in seven instructional videotapes. Named Best Billiard Writer by *Billiards Digest*, Byrne lives in Dubuque, Iowa.

About the Series Editor

Luc Sante is a renowned writer and critic, and author of the classic book on the raffish, violent, and criminal side of New York, *Low Life*. He also wrote the introduction for Anchor Books's reissue of the David Maurer classic, *The Big Con*. An authority on the history of photography, Sante is now a professor at Bard College.

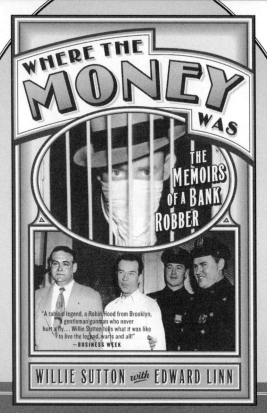

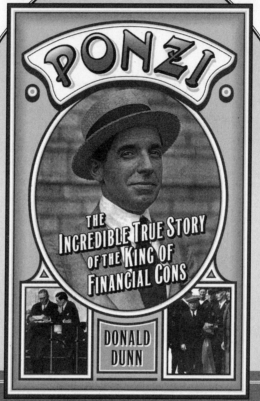